I0071911

The AEC Professional's Guidebook:
70 Lessons to a Stronger Career

By Gabe Lett

Copyright © 2021 by Gabe Lett

All rights reserved.

Cover designed by: Tony Otero of A.M. Otero Creative

Edited by: Jami Carpenter, www.redpengirl.com

No part of this publication may be reproduced, distributed, or transmitted in any form or by any means, including photocopying, recording, or other electronic or mechanical methods, without the prior written permission of the publisher, except in the case of brief quotations embodied in critical reviews and certain other noncommercial uses permitted by copyright law.

Printed in the United States of America

ISBN-13 978-0-578-30452-6

"The title of Gabe Lett's new book is spot-on. We've seen too many manuscripts stuffed with platitudes and philosophies. This book, however, truly is THE guidebook for success and distinction for A/E/C professionals! It is chock-full of real-world, practical, actionable strategies. Read it ... and prosper from the iconic insights that Gabe delivers so remarkably."

– Scott McKain, www.scottmckain.com, Author of *The Collapse of Distinction: Stand Out and Move Up While Your Competition Fails.*

"Gabe Lett, in his new book, *The AEC Professional's Guidebook: 70 Lessons to a Stronger Career,* lays out practically everything anyone would need to know to become a more successful marketing professional working in an AEC firm today. Every AEC marketer should read it. I also think many of those who own and manage AEC firms could benefit from the content and logical thought process Gabe lays out in his book. They, too, need to understand the fundamentals of marketing and business development, content marketing, how to communicate better, and how to become better leaders of marketing and better leaders of their firms.

I like Gabe's writing style. It is clear, coherent ... and thankfully devoid of the clichés and buzz terms that would set off the BS detectors of any sensible marketer or design professional today."

– Mark C. Zweig, Founder & Chairman, Zweig Group

"In the world of building stuff, we always need fresh perspectives and wisdom outside ourselves to keep our businesses thriving. In particular, most AEC companies are led by technical professionals who do the work. As such, we need to listen to voices outside our realms of expertise to sharpen our leadership and guide us in building our businesses. Gabe Lett has given us seventy lessons to do just that. When it comes to building a stronger career, Gabe has written and compiled a robust guidebook. I strongly encourage anyone working in the AEC industry to put these lessons into practice. If you do, your career will grow and your business will improve."

– Craig Galati, FAIA, FSMPS, CPSM, Principal at LGA Architecture, Author of *The Reluctant Leader*

"Gabe does a brilliant job synthesizing a wide array of knowledge into a book that is rich with critical insights and valuable lessons. His lessons are crisp, clear, and immediately actionable. A worthy investment for any AEC professional."

– JonRobert Tartaglione, Founder and CEO, Influence 51, Author of *The Neuropsychology of Influence and Decision-Making*

So many times, effective and impactful change begins as with timely reminder. In *The AEC Professionals Guidebook: 70 Lessons to a Stronger Career*, Gabe Lett shares best marketing practices in a clear, concise voice that easily resonates with A/E/C marketers and technically trained colleagues alike. Born from his own journey to improve his team's skills, Gabe provides thoughtful and impactful lessons that will benefit your firm and your career. Read it, highlight and mark pages, and refer to it often!

– Donna Corlew, FSMPS, CPSM, Chief Whatever It Takes Officer, C*Connect

"I don't think it's an exaggeration to say Gabe Lett's *The AEC Professional's Guidebook: 70 Lessons to a Stronger Career* is a modern-day marketing bible for marketing, business development, and technical professionals. There is no shortage of books about marketing, sales, leadership, professional development, project management, and effective writing but, like the Bible, this book encapsulates all of them, plus 70 relevant lessons, into one easy-to-use reference tool for AEC professionals at all levels of their career. Every firm should buy a copy for each member of their professional staff and compare 'Gabe's way' to their internal processes. I encourage every reader to follow Gabe's lead and use his book to help build others up."

– Carla Thompson, FSMPS, CPSM, Senior Marketing Consultant, Elevate Marketing Advisors, Weld Coxe Marketing Achievement Award (2018)

Dedication

For all the friends I have made through the Society for Marketing Professional Services (SMPS). Your loyalty and commitment to the A/E/C marketing profession are the foundation from which this work has grown!

CONTENTS

Acknowledgments

A SPECIAL THANK YOU to several voices who helped shape this contribution.

Thank you to my employer, Allgeier, Martin and Associates. Your receptivity and openness to always improving our marketing make my work enjoyable.

Thank you Carla Thompson, Donna Corlew, and Craig Galati. The three of you reviewed the manuscript and encouraged me to publish this material. Your insights and guidance are appreciated.

Thank you, Dad, for inviting me into this world of marketing A/E/C services. Your belief in me to effect change in your engineering firm started me on this journey.

Introduction

IT WAS MONDAY, AUGUST 19, and I'd been at my new job for almost a year. Allgeier, Martin, and Associates is a civil and electrical consulting engineering firm for whom I was directing marketing activities. I had spent most of that first year reviewing the company's marketing collateral. As I read project descriptions, resumes, website copy, and cover letters, I identified several areas for improvement. The readability was extremely difficult. The language was technical and impersonal. So, I set out to rewrite the majority of copy I was reviewing.

Fortunately, I had very little pushback. The firm's leaders and project managers seemed all too happy to have me rewrite content to make it more accessible. I split long run-on sentences into two or three. I removed redundant clauses and simplified weak 'to be' verbs with stronger, more punchy verbs. Then, on August 19, I had an epiphany.

If my colleagues continued to write in the same manner, I would forever be making these edits and improving new marketing copy. What could I do to improve my colleagues' writing? As with most initiatives, I was too audacious at the beginning. I dreamed of training workshops and how-to videos. But my audacity quickly faded in the realization that one, I would never have enough time to properly develop and execute writing seminars, and two, my colleagues would most likely not be interested in investing much time and energy into learning how to write better.

So, with my intentions tempered, I decided to craft a little marketing tip about writing that I would email my colleagues.

I wanted to start small and keep it simple. My idea was to email a new marketing tip every Monday morning. It would be a slow-drip campaign for improving my colleagues' writing skills over time. I felt they would accept the simplicity and short nature of the emails and I would accomplish my objective, just at a slower pace. But what would I write about first? What could be a very easy fix that anyone could do?

I landed on correcting the 'double-spaced period.' Many of my coworkers had been trained to type on typewriters, not word processing software. I, too, was of an age when the technology for creating written documents was changing. In junior high, I was taught keyboarding on a typewriter. In high school, we made the jump to computers and word processing software. I learned to double space after a period but had to re-learn to use only a single space a few years later.

(For those of you reading this book who are confused about the double-spaced period, it is true you only need to single space after a period when writing in word processing software. Jump to Lesson 61 for a full explanation.)

So, I wrote out a 184-word marketing tip about why we now use a single-space after a period. The tip went into an email that Monday morning.

Monday Marketing Tips

The tip about the double-spaced period was a hit. Many staff approached me later that day and during the week thanking me for the tip. There were several water-cooler conversations about typewriters and computers and who learned what and when. I had immediate confirmation that I had stumbled onto something valuable. I also noticed a slow change in the documents I received in that double spacing after a period was starting to diminish.

Because of the success of the Monday Morning Marketing Tip email, I decided to make it a habit. At first, I thought the tips would all have to do with writing. But I discovered a one-dimensional topic may not hold attention very long. I quickly decided to write tips about other topics, mostly having to do with marketing and business development. Thus, the Monday Marketing Tip campaign was born!

If you look at the Table of Contents of this book, you will notice many lessons—seventy, to be exact—are all adapted from Monday Marketing Tips. Somewhere along the way, I noticed my collection of tips was getting long and covered a variety of great A/E/C business topics. It reminded me of a book I had read for my counseling license, *The Gift of Therapy: An Open Letter to a New Generation of Therapists and Their Patients*, by Irvin Yalom. The purpose of Yalom's book was a collection of wisdom, guidance, and advice from a seasoned therapist to beginning therapists. It struck a chord!

How to Read and Process This Book

Like Yalom's *The Gift of Therapy*, I am offering a collection of wisdom, guidance, and advice from seasoned A/E/C marketers to beginning and entry-level marketers, as well as technical staff. I have discovered that I often go back to Yalom's deep wells of understanding to continue to learn and grow as a therapist. I believe this book provides the same opportunity for veteran A/E/C professionals.

As with most collections, please do not feel the constraints of reading this book in sequential order. While that is certainly not a bad way to read this book, you may discover that jumping to your favorite topics or the areas in which you wish to improve will serve you well. The content is organized in a way to make it easy for you to find what interests you.

I am not the only author, as I have leaned on, borrowed from, and gleaned a great deal from other A/E/C marketers and leaders. Their content is carefully noted and credited. I encourage you to explore the references at the end of this book.

Thank you for reading this book. I trust its contents will bring value to your career!

Chapter 1 – Marketing

Lesson 1: Content Marketing

"Sometimes referred to as education-based marketing, inbound marketing, or thought leadership marketing, the idea behind content marketing is to provide interesting, useful information – aka 'content' – to your target audience." (Scott D. Butcher, FSMPS, CPSM, www.aecumen.com) [1]

With the advent of the internet, accompanied by the information age, there has come content marketing. Now content marketing is nothing new. Before the information age, presenting at a conference, writing an article or whitepaper, or contributing to a panel discussion were all the same concepts. You share your expertise and knowledge with others to generate interest in hiring you to perform architecture, engineering, or construction services. This is the essence of good content marketing. But now there is a much larger and more consistent platform from which to share your expertise and knowledge.

A brief story will illustrate the power of content marketing. The window regulator broke in my car door causing the window to stay open permanently. I needed to fix it but did not want to pay for expensive body shop labor. I went to YouTube and searched for a 'how-to' video to replace my window regulator. The body shop expert demonstrated step-by-step how to complete this easy repair. In the process, he recommended the best places to buy a quality replacement part online or in a local auto parts store. After reviewing several options, I purchased the part online. I then watched the video as I replaced the regulator, saving myself several hundred dollars.

I made a purchase decision based on the online know-how of a body shop expert who posted a 'how-to' video on YouTube. While engineering services are much more complex and expensive, the same strategy applies. Utilizing social media channels, blogs, infographics, ebooks, and more, engineers can demonstrate their expertise and position themselves as leading experts in their fields.

The primary objection to content or thought leadership marketing is that A/E/C professionals do not like to give away their ideas, tactics, or methods for free. While this is of concern, there is a right way and wrong way to deliver good content.

The wrong way is to share trade secrets or specific processes that differentiate your services from your competitors. This is content I believe should be reserved for paying clients. However, there are many topics on which you can deliver value without compromising your ability to bill for your services. And I promise that for every professional who stands in front of an audience or delivers a quick video online about something that everyone in her profession does, dozens of others will not. This is the secret to successful content marketing. If you are delivering something of value that very few, if any, of your competitors are delivering, you have automatically differentiated yourself as the expert on that topic.

You also need to look at this from the perspective of the

professional who is not utilizing content marketing. If you are one of the dozens of 'other' professionals who are not delivering anything of value to clients and prospects for free, you have successfully identified yourself as 'just another engineer.' You've given no reason for someone to consider your services or trust you with their project. They will likely go to the guy who helped them solve something small from a video they saw on LinkedIn.

Challenge

If you are not utilizing content marketing, start small. Get active on LinkedIn and start posting things you are passionate about in your job. It doesn't have to be original content from your brain. You can deliver good stuff from others (non-competitors), and still be received as someone who can help. Set a goal to propose educational content at a professional association conference next year. Offer to write a piece as a guest to blogs you follow. Do something to get noticed for your expertise by giving little pieces of it away in the right places.

Lesson 2: Marketing 2022 Highlights

A recent survey conducted by the Society for Marketing Professional Services (SMPS) Foundation revealed some interesting trends and forecasts in A/E/C marketing. Marketing 2022[2] is a survey exploring current and future A/E/C marketing practices. There were 330 responses to the SMPS survey in the first quarter 2019. Of the 330 responses, 29% were from engineering firms, 22% construction, 16% architecture, 18% architecture/engineering, 12% other, and 3% geotechnical or environmental. Here are some of the more interesting results.

- The top five marketing approaches predicted by 2022 are:

- **Client Experience**: Ongoing activities for engaging clients and collecting feedback—then reacting to that feedback as appropriate.

- **Networking**: Engaging in events, trade shows, and similar business gatherings to build and maintain professional relationships from which to give and receive referrals.

- **Thought Leadership**: Various methods of providing insight into the talents and knowledge base of your organization (presentations, blogging, publishing, whitepapers, webinars, etc.)

- **Branding**: The set of experiences, memories, stories, and relationships that, taken together, account for a consumer's decision to choose one firm over another.

- **Content Marketing**: Closely aligned with thought leadership, education-based content delivered to increase awareness, consideration, and decision phases of the buying process.

- 70% of respondents stated they believe competition will increase over the next three years. This is a wake-up call that a new norm is in the industries; price pressures will continue.

- 70% of survey participants noted that their firms are currently utilizing **Thought Leadership Marketing**. By 2022, 80% believe their firms will be utilizing this approach.

- Only 18% of firms represented in the survey currently have an in-place **Client Experience Strategy**, and yet, Client Experience was projected to become the top marketing approach by 2022. *Note: Clients are no longer handing work directly to design firms. Instead, they're increasingly requiring three proposals, or even going* *through a drawn-out prequalification process, and then asking the prequalified firms in their database to submit proposals.*

- The easiest sale to make is an existing service to an existing client. The most difficult service to sell is a new service to a new client.

- Firms who value their relationships and place a high level of emphasis on enhancing the quality of their client interactions will experience growth and lead the way in **Client Experience Marketing**.

- Roughly 61% of firms who have not refreshed their **Branding** in the past three years, plan to do so over the next three years.

  - Related to the firm's **Branding**, a **Personal Brand** is the perception a person has of an individual within the firm. Much like the mid-20th century architect or engineer-of-record, a professional's **Personal Brand** is becoming more important and effective in winning work.

  - **Personal Brands** are becoming more effective because of the rise in **Social Media Networking** and **Thought Leadership Marketing** delivered by videos, webinars, articles, and the like via social media and websites.

Additional topics addressed in the survey included podcasting, video marketing, corporate culture, account-based marketing, personal selling, proposal automation, lead generating websites, client relationship management (CRM) software, marketing, and business development top skills.

For me, the biggest takeaways from this research were the heavy emphasis on thought leadership/content marketing and the rise in client experience as a major focus for retaining and growing clients. In both areas, interactions with the client are placed at a high priority. What this tells me is that clients are desiring more interaction and collaboration with architects, engineers, and contractors.

We are not too many decades removed from the time in this industry when A/E/C professionals were hired and then left alone to put their brilliance to work designing and building. Once they completed their tasks, the client was informed, and deliverables were delivered. But today's clients have become much more sophisticated. The abundance of connectivity online and ease of travel give clients the ability to expect more interaction and collaboration. They are no longer satisfied with an end product. They want to see how it's made, learn something, and have some input. Therefore, A/E/C professionals who up their client-relationship game by providing greater thought leadership and taking their clients on an enjoyable and educational journey will be winning most of the work.

Challenge

Considering the top five marketing approaches predicted for 2022, which of these five make the biggest impact on you and why? What are you going to do about it? Your challenge is to take at least one of these top five marketing approaches and implement something new or different in your firm. I chose to introduce a client survey program.

Lesson 3: Taking Marketing Photos

Many of you take construction site photos before, during, and after a project. Most of these photos are for purposes such as gathering site data, inspections, and closeouts. Sometimes, you may take a photo that accidentally is good for marketing purposes. However, most of the photos have no marketing value. Here are some tips for taking good marketing photos while on a project site.

Quality

The first aspect to consider is the quality of the camera you are using. Most of you likely use your smartphone for project photos. While this is not ideal, it can be a good quality photo if you know how to use your smartphone camera appropriately. A few easy things to remember include;

- Do not use your zoom-in feature, which diminishes quality
- It's best to use the default photo setting
- In some smartphones, you can touch your screen in various sections to change the brightness settings as you see fit.

If you want to increase the quality of your photos, learn how to use a decent digital camera. Take some quick courses online or buy a photography 'how-to' book. However, the best camera is the one you have with you. Learn more about the tools you already have to get the best quality out of them.

Composition

Composing a great marketing photo is not as difficult as you may think. There are a few simple rules to composing a great photo.

- View your photo in thirds. This means looking at the view and adjusting it to capture three significant subjects in equal thirds (i.e., roadway, sky, trees).
- Look for unique and unconventional angles. Try to position yourself and your view at an angle typically not seen from the natural eye.

- Get as close to your subject as possible without losing the context. This takes some practice, but when you get it right you will know by the results.

Like any skill, composing a great photo takes practice. The good news is you have a digital camera on you at all times on your smartphone. You can practice all you want without wasting film.

Volume

Don't be afraid to take too many pictures. Because the photos are digital, you are not wasting film. Sometimes you must take eight or ten shots of the same subject to get one really great photo. That's fine. Whatever you take, be sure to save ALL the photos and share them with your marketing staff.

Depending on the project and its marketing value, your best decision may be to spend a little money and hire a professional photographer. If you do, make sure to hire a photographer who regularly shoots landscapes, buildings, and infrastructure. Be sure to ask to see some of their work. If they will let you, request to go on their shoot with them, and don't be afraid to share your ideas. It is also an opportunity for you to learn how to take better pictures.

Challenge

Take a half-day and go shoot several projects. Practice composing the pictures and taking them at different times of the day and in various weather patterns. Try looking for unique and fun perspectives. Review competitor websites and look for pictures and graphics that grab your attention. Study these and make note of how they are composed, what colors are popping, what is the perspective or angle.

Lesson 4: Cross-Marketing

What is cross-marketing? Cross-marketing is effective if the firm has a diversity of services lines, clients, and geographic footprint. Most A/E/C firms have several business lines or even divisions of expertise. Cross-marketing is more challenging for smaller niche firms that most often are sub-consultants.

The consulting engineers for whom I work offer a variety of service lines in both electric power delivery and civil public works. These are further diversified into electric transmission and distribution, communications, water and wastewater systems, roads, and bridges, and more. We also have a diversity of clients from electric coops to public or private water utilities and Native American tribes. Our geographic footprint covers a Midwest region of six states with five offices. We are a prime candidate for effective cross-marketing!

In short, cross-marketing is promoting other lines of business than your own to a current and satisfied client. For example, if I am a civil engineer working for a regional wastewater utility, I may have a chat with my client about the capabilities of the electrical control staff at my firm. This would benefit my client because of their need for electrical controls at their treatment plant as well as pumping stations within the collection system.

A primary key to effective cross-marketing is a 'one-company' culture. This means that all staff members are aware of the diverse service lines, clients, and geographic footprint. Not only are all staff aware, but they should be able to speak intelligently about all of it. A one-company culture recognizes that when other design teams and service lines in my company do well, I do well, too. More importantly, if I can bring highly skilled experts to my client in another area other than my own, I have brought value to my client and solidified trust.

When everyone in the company is regularly thinking about the 'other' services outside of their silo, the foundation for cross-marketing effectiveness is established. This takes an effort to regularly communicate and educate the entire company on everything we do under our brand.

In summary, cross-marketing is talking about and promoting multiple services with existing clients. It works best with clients who may need a variety of engineering services and are not aware of the other services our firm has to offer that may be of value to them. A perfect cross-marketing example for my firm is an electric coop client. This client is primarily served by our Electric T&D and Substation teams. However, this same client has hired our Civil Department staff to complete storm water and structural projects at their headquarters facility.

Stay informed of what other teams and departments are accomplishing. Promote a 'one-company' culture and let's help each other grow!

Challenge

Make a list of your clients you believe are good cross-marketing targets. Narrow that list down to three and develop a cross-marketing plan to grow those targeted clients with services they have not yet hired.

Lesson 5: Simplicity in Marketing

Several years ago, I read a good business marketing book, *Collapse of Distinction*, by Scott McKain.[3] One of the ideas in his book that stuck with me was the concept of distilling your message—what you are about—to its simplest form. Too many businesses and professionals are stuck in a sea of sameness. It becomes difficult for clients to distinguish one engineering firm from another. Here is a very brief example.

While working for another firm, I had the official title of Vice President for Marketing and Business Development. That was a mouthful and I quickly tired of having to repeat it. Besides, no one ever remembered it, because there was nothing memorable or distinct about that title. I decided to put 'Marketing Guy' as the title on my business card. It was simple, clear, and direct. As far as I knew, no one else in the industry was using this title. It was remarkable how quickly that simple change in my title made me memorable and elicited positive responses. Even to this day, I occasionally run into someone I have not seen for several years, who will say, "I remember you. You're the Marketing Guy!"

The best marketing harnesses what you do and creates a memorable and distinctive message. Consider how you present yourself and your work. Get rid of the tired phrases of sameness and infuse new and creative ways of introducing yourself. Instead of, "I'm an electrical engineer. I design electric transmission and distribution lines, substations, etc.," consider, "I make sure your lights stay on. I deliver power!" Which of these two introductions are more likely to elicit a positive response and possibly more interest?

We recently changed our introduction on the www.amce.com homepage to, 'Safe, Reliable, and Sensible Engineering Solutions.' Rather than tell people we are two divisions—civil and electrical—how many people work here, and what disciplines of engineering we practice … yadda, yadda, yadda, it is much more memorable and compelling to state what we do briefly and simply.

Challenge

Audit your marketing collateral and language, starting with your website. In this audit look for meaningless boring language that everyone uses and consider alternative language that is simple and memorable. Keep the language in line with your brand and the authentic identity of your company. Use your creativity and don't be afraid to ask others for their ideas as well. Once you have sifted through your web pages, move on to brochures, cover letters, project descriptions, etc. Good marketing is memorable. Do something and say something memorable!

Lesson 6: Improve Your Batting Average

As most of you know, a batting average is the approximate percentage of time a batter will get a base hit when at-bat. If baseball players are successful at getting a base hit 30% of the time (Avg. .300), they are among the best hitters in the game. For A/E/C business, our batting average is called the "hit rate." Specifically, for engineering firms, a hit rate of 33%–38% is average in the industry, depending on what research you review.

A firm's hit rate is calculated by dividing the total number of project wins by the total number of proposals/qualifications submitted (wins/total proposals = hit rate). For example, if your firm has won 11 projects out of 24 proposals submitted your hit rate is 46%. So what practices should you employ to continue to improve your batting average or hit rate?

1. The best opportunities for project wins come with a long lead time. When we know an RFQ or RFP is coming before it is published, the hit rate jumps to 68%. For RFQs/RFPs we responded to but did not know were coming, our hit rate falls to 25%. The best practice is to limit our responses to RFQs/RFPs we know about ahead of time. *(This data is unique to my company. However, it is subjectively true across the A/E/C industry)*

2. When you do have a project lead, you should do your best to qualify that lead as a good project. Qualify the lead by:

   a. examining construction/engineering value,

   b. determining who is best to be project manager or point-of-contact,

   c. history of work with the client,

   d. financial stability of the client and funding for the project,

   e. availability of staff (time and talent) to complete a successful project.

3. Utilize your CRM to track and qualify leads, and hold your business development staff accountable for regular follow up. Establishing long-lasting relationships is the best method for securing future work.

4. Use data to make go/no-go decisions. If the data demonstrate a low probability of a win, you should seriously consider passing on the opportunity. It is okay to use your gut and respond contrary to the data, but you should consider the workload of your marketing staff and be able to defend your decision.

Finally, track your revenue volume hit rate. Revenue volume hit rate is determined by dividing the revenue of projects won by the total revenue of projects submitted. Your revenue volume hit rate is 39% if you have won $3,244,926 divided by $8,406,651 total submitted. This is a good measure to track to make sure you are winning valuable projects, not just smaller revenue projects.

It is good practice to track both hit rate by count or number of projects won as well as hit rate by volume of revenue. These two key performance indicators (KPIs) should tell you a story about how well your firm is doing in your proposal and qualifications presentation and if the projects are generating enough revenue.

Challenge

If you haven't already, start tracking your count and volume hit rates. If you have a robust CRM, it will usually track these KPIs for you. If you do not, you may still track it on a simple spreadsheet. No matter how you do it, be sure you are doing it and sharing this data with your leadership. This kind of data can promote necessary changes in your project pursuits, proposal processes, and business development practices. It can also validate your marketing leadership and assist your firm in working smarter!

Lesson 7: Brand Consistency

Branding is the set of experiences, memories, stories, and relationships that, taken together, account for a consumer's decision to choose one firm over another. Branding is not a company's logo, colors, style, or voice. However, there is a relationship between visible appearance (logo, colors, style, voice) and a company's true 'brand.' Clients will associate what they feel and think about your firm with your visible branding. For this reason, consistency in your visible appearance and voice is important.

At my firm, in 2020, the marketing team initiated a brand audit. We began collecting samples of client-facing documents, graphics, images, etc., to assess if our visible brand appearance was consistent. We believed most client-facing material was generally adhering to our brand style. However, it was no surprise to discover there were inconsistencies. I attached sample documents of brand inconsistency to an email for our leadership to review. The easiest and simplest way to correct brand inconsistencies is to periodically remind employees of our brand guidelines with examples. Our team asked employees to take several minutes to review correctly branded documents. If the employee discovered brand inconsistencies (business cards, email signature, letterhead, etc.), we asked them to please take steps to correct those inconsistencies. We also offered to assist in creating correctly branded templates, if needed.

We made sure to ask employees to work with their supervisors before making any changes to shared documents or templates. These included meeting agendas, reports, work authorization agreements, contracts, and other commonly used and shared documents. We asked them NOT to make changes to these types of documents without consulting their supervisor!

This exercise caught some fairly egregious brand violations. It did not perfect everything, but our audit made significant improvements! Specifically, we discovered some PowerPoint presentations that were using a company logo and tagline from the early 1980s!

Challenge

Plan and execute a brand audit with your leadership's approval and buy-in. Be prepared to find some heart-dropping brand breaches. Also, be prepared to have to do some work to create branded templates that are well-communicated and easy to access.

Lesson 8: Determine Your Brand

When clients, business associates, and prospects think of (insert your company here), what comes to their minds? Of course, it is not the same for everyone. Depending on their interactions with your firm and people, the answers will vary. However, there are likely several thoughts that are consistent around themes. What clients, business associates, and prospects think about you forms your true brand.

We only discover these thoughts and themes if these people choose to share them with us. Client surveys, debriefs, typical project interactions, and secondhand information are all sources that can reveal what others think of us.

The more important question is this: "What do we *want* our clients, business associates, and prospects to think of our firm and our people?" For my consulting engineering company, I recommend that most, if not all, our clients wish for a safe, reliable, and sensible solution to their engineering problems. What about your company? What are some of the key ingredients that all or most of your clients desire when they work with your people?

When engineering infrastructure, safety is number one. Whatever we are designing must prove safe. Once safety is secure, reliability is a very close second. Will the infrastructure reliably perform? Can the owner trust your designed project to do what it is supposed to do and do it consistently? Finally, most owners want a safe and reliable project that is delivered sensibly. Project costs and the time to complete it must be reasonable, sensible.

After this brand-mapping exercise, we launched a new marketing initiative to utilize these three adjectives consistently. Over the next few months, our proposals, qualifications statements, cover letters, website, social media posts, and marketing collateral utilized these three adjectives. We wanted our fans and soon-to-be fans to think safe, reliable, sensible when they think of my firm, Allgeier, Martin, and Associates.

Challenge

Is your brand message consistent throughout all the external and internal communications of your company? Do you even have a consistent brand message? Your challenge is to either develop a consistent brand message or better utilize your brand message in ALL marketing collateral and internal communications.

Lesson 9: Marketing Goals

Occasionally, it is fun to get in the car and drive with no particular place to go. However, most days, you get in your car with a plan. You need to get to a specific location, so you think about your route, traffic, and preferences. You then execute your plan to get to your goal.

Some think of marketing as getting in the car and driving with no particular place to go. Let's drive and see where we end up. Let's respond to every RFQ and see what we win. Let's visit a bunch of prospective clients and see who hires us. Let's make brochures, put our logo on coffee mugs, attend as many conferences as we can afford, and see how many people wish to work with us. This is *not* marketing!

I established six specific marketing goals for 2020 to keep our marketing efforts focused and purposeful. These six goals established our route, assessed the traffic, and considered our business preferences.

1. Growth in geographic areas we have established office presence.
2. Increase project opportunities with existing clients through cross-marketing.
3. Refresh and strengthen our brand.
4. Increase client awareness of special areas of expertise and skill.
5. Increase client satisfaction and loyalty; decrease client turnover.
6. Be more efficient in RFQ responses and increase our hit rate.

Each of these goals has specific strategies for implementation. For example, we acquired a small two-man firm in a city with one of our branch offices. This served our goal to grow geographically (Goal #1). I have written a couple of Marketing Tip emails regarding cross-marketing and encouraged project managers to consider the firm's full range of services when working with a client (Goal #2). We have been performing client debriefs and engaged in a client satisfaction survey to increase client satisfaction and loyalty (Goal #5). Our hit rate in 2019 was 39%. We are currently (Q3, 2020) at a 48% hit rate and making better go/no-go decisions on RFQs (Goal #6).[4]

At the time of the initial writing of this Monday Marketing Tip, we were about halfway through 2020, doing well in achieving our goals. However, we still had the latter half of 2020 to continue meeting our goals. I proposed some additional strategies to execute for the remainder of the year.

Initiate some business development training for personnel in Kansas City, Rolla, and Springfield (Goal #1). Identify 'subject matter experts' (SMEs) within our firm and assist these SMEs in developing content to share with clients and prospects via a blogging platform and/or submitting articles in client publications (Goal #4).[5]

Keeping an eye on your goals and revisiting them at least once a quarter is a good practice. I have my six goals for 2020 printed and posted right behind my desk where I see them every day. Colleagues visiting my office stop and read my six goals and ask questions. But just having goals is not sufficient. You must think about strategies to execute to meet those goals. List those strategies along with your goals to keep you accountable.

Challenge

No matter where you are in the calendar year, stop

reading and revisit your marketing goals for the year. Or start developing your marketing goals if you do not have any. Keep your goals SMART: Specific, Measurable, Achievable, Relevant, Time-Bound. Keep your goals simple and short. Share your goals with leadership and ask for their input.

Lesson 10: Highest Proposal Differentiators

I recently read a research article titled, "Procurement of Architecture and Engineering Services: Influence of Cost on Selection Outcomes and Evaluation Criteria That Best Differentiate Consultant Expertise."[6] WOW, that's a mouthful!

In short, the article reviewed and ran statistical analyses on 122 publicly procured A/E projects in North America (consisting of 804 individual proposals). 102 proposals were evaluated using the guidelines of limited cost weighting and a two-envelope procedure. This procurement approach utilized a 'best value' approach by separating cost proposals from qualification criteria and scoring them separately. Twenty proposals were evaluated using a qualifications-based selection (QBS) method only.

There were several inferences made based on the analysis.

• The highest differentiators of evaluation criteria were schedule, cost, interview, and technical approach. These criteria demonstrated the most deviation of evaluator scoring.

• The consultant ranked first in related experience was selected 88% of the time!

• Selected consultants were placed, on average, first in the interview and related experience; second in cost, schedule, and technical proposals; and third in past performance.

- It can be concluded that the inclusion of cost as an evaluation criterion does have a disproportionate effect on selection outcomes, such that selections are slightly skewed toward the lowest bid or non-highest qualified consultant.

For a more thorough understanding, the article is referenced at the end of this book. My takeaway was to make sure we focus our proposals mostly on related experience, then do our best to create an efficient schedule and write a comprehensive technical approach. Because most of our civil proposals do not include an interview component, the best method for creating an interview is having a pre-existing relationship with the client as well as a physical site visit and discussion of the project.

Not all clients or projects differentiate the same criteria. For some, the schedule will take priority. For others, it may be staff with very similar technical experience. The goal for the marketer is to discover what is driving the project and selection of a consultant with each client and project pursuit.

Challenge

Take several of these proposal elements and figure out how to ask the right go/no-go questions to elicit the project drivers. Review your go/no-go process and make sure you are asking the right questions and weighing the score to match the more important proposal components. Do not get locked into the same go/no-go process or project pursuit strategy for every proposal. Be fluid and flexible so your processes align well with each client and project.

Lesson 11: Storytelling

What makes for great marketing are great stories! Every marketing professional will tell you, no matter the form of delivery or amount of money spent, if a customer does not remember your message and repeat it, it is likely not very effective marketing. People will remember and repeat great stories. Therefore, storytelling is the strongest and most effective way to market.

Your best marketing are the stories you tell about your job, your projects, your challenges. What stories do you have to tell? Every good story has seven (7) key elements.

1. The Character: There is always a main character, who is the hero. Make sure your work stories place your client in the role of the main character and hero.

2. The Problem: The hero runs into a challenge or obstacle. This is the problem of your story.

3. The Guide: The hero meets a guide who provides wisdom and assistance to overcome the problem. You, the design professional, are the guide.

4. The Plan: The guide offers a plan that will help the hero overcome their problem.

5. The Challenge: Once a plan is laid out for the hero, the guide must call the hero to action. This call to action is the hero's challenge.

6. The Failure Avoidance: Once the hero engages the challenge, the guide helps them avoid failure.

7. The Success: The hero overcomes the problem and experiences success. The hero's life is changed for the better.

No matter what marketing medium we choose, the messages we give must relate to the stories of our clients. We cannot tell a fully developed story in the short marketing timeframes available. However, marketing best practices are to think of our messages as part of the fully developed stories. These messages, over time, help our clients understand the full story.

For a more thorough examination of the seven key

elements of a good story, pick up a copy of Don Miller's book, *Building A Story Brand*.[7] Having read Miller's book and implemented a host of new marketing messages, I can testify to the power of great storytelling. The more our industry leans into video, client experience, thought leadership, and content marketing, the more valuable good storytelling will be.

Challenge

Find three to five project descriptions that are key projects of your firm. Rewrite those project descriptions as stories using the seven elements of good storytelling. Write the stories first without regard to length or formatting. Just write and allow your creativity to breathe. Once written, read through your stories several times, then try and tell the story verbally. Now, go back and format the stories into a framework that will work for your marketing collateral.

Lesson 12: The Guide, Not The Hero

In the last lesson, I introduced the idea of storytelling as one of your strongest marketing tools. You may wish to review Lesson 11 as you consider this lesson.

The most common error many marketers and engineering professionals make when telling their company's story is placing themselves in the role of hero. I cannot emphasize this enough: the *client* is the hero of the story! When you make yourself or your firm the *hero*, the client loses interest in your story. Besides, when most other competing firms are making themselves the heroes, you simply sound like everyone else. Nothing differentiates you or makes your story memorable. You are the guide who assists the hero. You are Yoda and the client is Luke Skywalker.

When telling the stories of your projects, the challenges

and obstacles you've overcome, the problems you've solved, turn the story toward the client and talk about the challenges *they* overcame and the problems you helped *them* solve.

This may take some extra courage to present to your leadership. For decades, the stories of A/E/C firms have been ego-centric placing our brilliant design professionals as the heroes of their own stories. This must flip! Besides, who doesn't want to be Yoda?

Challenge

Revisit the challenge of Lesson 11. Audit those stories to make sure you have framed the client as the *hero* and your design pros as the *guide*. If the story is well-written, hooking the interest and emotion of the reader, I am confident your leadership will see the value.

Lesson 13: Making Good Go/No-Go Decisions

When we receive a request for proposal or qualifications (RFP/RFQ), marketing best practices indicate the need for a robust 'go or no-go' discussion. It seems obvious that throwing our qualifications and marketing resources at everything is a bad idea. However, the temptation is extraordinarily powerful to think we can win nearly every proposal when reality dictates this is illogical.

According to Zweig Group, PSMJ, and SMPS research, the industry average win rate hovers between 40%–45%. That means an average engineering firm will lose 55%–60% of the projects for which they compete against other firms. Even high-performing firms barely get to a 50% win rate. The unicorns that year-over-year win over 50% of their competitive proposals are typically small niche firms, not multi-disciplined firms.

The hit rate from the past three years at my firm tells a

clear story. When we do make good no-go decisions our win rates (both number and revenue volume) go up.

- 2019: No-go decision for eight (8) RFQs.
  - o   37% Win Rate (Number)
  - o   35% Win Rate (Volume)
- 2020: No-go decision for twenty-two (22) RFQs
  - o   52% Win Rate (Number)
  - o   45% Win Rate (Volume)
- 2021: No-go Decision for ten (10) RFQs
  - o   43% Win Rate (Number)
  - o   28% Win Rate (Volume)

The numbers tell us that when we make better no-go decisions, we win more work and better revenue work. So what is involved in making good go/no-go decisions?

The most valid and reliable information in predicting a win on a competitive proposal is whether or not the firm knew about the RFP/RFQ before it was published. The reason this metric is such a good indicator is that it assumes a pre-existing relationship and good business development practices. People choose to work with people they know and trust. If the owner does not know you, how can they decide to trust you?

Secondary indicators to consider in the go/no-go decision include:

- Client's ability to fund the project and collaborate on the design.
- We understand what is 'driving' this project and what problem it will solve.
- We know the decision-makers well and they know us.
- We understand who our competitors are and we can demonstrate equal or better technical qualifications

than the competitors.

- We have the capacity, available staff, and resources to complete the project equal to or exceeding the client's expectations.

- We have adequate time to put together a high-quality and tailored proposal.

These are some of the most important factors in making the go/no-go decision. Many firms formalize this process by creating point values to these factors to help them establish statistical odds of winning. Others simply ask themselves specific questions regarding these factors to get a subjective sense of what decision to make.

Regardless of whether the strategy is formalized into a point system or more subjective for discussion, the value of having a go/no-go process is in making the best use of your marketing resources to win valuable work.

Challenge

If you are at a company that is *not* using a go/no-go process, it is time to introduce one. This may prove a difficult task if the decision-makers have a long history of making these decisions from their gut. Keeping this in mind, go slow and be patient. You may wish to craft a formal go/no-go process for yourself and apply it to your RFQ/RFP responses for a year. Gather the data to see how accurately you can predict the wins and losses with your go/no-go process.

I am still doing this at my firm because I have some naysayers and some buy-ins. Our go/no-go process is not utilized 100%. When I make a go decision based on my process we win 92% of the time. When I make a no-go decision based on my process we win 13% of the time. There is a small 'gray' area where the decision could go either way and we win those 33% of the time. I am building the case to institute my formal process based on data.

Lesson 14: In Rainbows

One of my favorite bands is Radiohead. My favorite album of theirs is *In Rainbows*. Why am I telling you this? Because of the marketing genius of the band's lead singer, Thom York, and producer, Nigel Godrich, the In Rainbows album was a smashing success and a huge seller. What did they do?

Great marketing often means doing something disruptive and surprising. The music industry in 2007 was in a major shift from the purchase of CDs to online digital streaming and downloads. Much of the online trading of music was illegal, but it was having a major impact on the record labels' and artists' ability to make money. So, Thom York and Nigel Godrich decided to self-release the record on their website. They offered the new album as a digital MP3 download with a pay-what-you-want trade model. This allowed the band to bypass a recording contract and remain stuck in the record company's stranglehold on when and how to release an album. The band was doing business directly with their customers and allowing their customers to determine the value of their product.

The result was three million downloads in the first year and a cool $10 million in revenue, by far, the band's biggest commercial success ever! You can read more from Wikipedia here https://bit.ly/39jiUMm.

Marketing takeaways:

o You still have to produce great work that your fans (clients) will love! The album is terrific.

o When you have an established fan base (client base), removing middlemen and obstacles so you can work directly for your clients increases loyalty and affinity for your brand.

o When your market is experiencing significant disruptions, embrace the disruptions and utilize them to your advantage.

o Allow your fans (clients) to determine the value of your product (service). Value-based pricing is a higher risk-reward tactic, but when you are confident in your service, the revenue should follow.

Challenge

Do you know who your biggest fans are? Which of your clients sing your firm's praises and refer business to you? These are the clients you want to innovate with when it comes to disruptive and surprising marketing tactics. To the technical staff, this may seem counterintuitive. "They are wonderful clients so let's not do anything to disrupt the relationship!" I argue that these clients love you already and you have built up tremendous loyalty. Doing something a little different is not going to push them away that easily.

With your biggest fans, what can you do differently to remove middlemen and obstacles in your work? How can you make it easier for your clients to work with you? What disruptions in your market can you embrace and utilize to your advantage? How can you structure your fees for your best clients so they are paying for the value you add to their organization?

Chapter 2 – Leadership

Lesson 15: You Be Nice!

Mark Cuban said, "One of the most underrated skills in business right now is being nice."[8]

That's right! Nice sells.

Your IQ and engineering skills got you your degree, but EQ and soft skills will get you paid! EQ is your Emotional Intelligence and refers to several abilities. The ability to control your emotions, read others' emotions correctly, adapt behavior, be curious and learn, execute self-discipline, accept rejection/failure, and others make up your EQ.

So, here are a few tips on increasing your EQ to match your already high IQ.

Tip #1 – Be responsive. Give your clients and colleagues feedback. Let them know your thoughts, progress, ideas, intuitions, goals, etc. Most left-brainers deal in facts only. Use your right brain and talk with clients about the big picture of what they wish to accomplish. Listen and let them know you hear them.

Tip #2 – Utilize the 10:10:10 rule. Before deciding or reacting in a negative emotion, consider the consequences of your decision or reaction ten minutes from now, ten months, and then ten years. What ripple effect could your angry words have not just in the short term, but in the long term?

Tip #3 – Practice scenarios of what could go wrong with a project or client. Imagine yourself having to respond to mistakes, errors, poor contractor performance, angry council members, or utility staff. Create responses that will de-escalate problems and bring calm to a situation.

Tip #4 – Do not assume you know the best solution. Ask lots of questions and take in information from your clients and colleagues. Have a humble and teachable attitude.

Tip #5 – When you experience rejection or failure, ask what you could have done differently to achieve a better outcome. Your instinct will be to blame something or someone external to yourself. Train yourself to first respond by questioning yourself and how you could have created a different outcome.

Unlike IQ, EQ can be learned and improved significantly, regardless of your baseline. There are signs that you need to improve your EQ. Have you lost a job or been disciplined for a lack of self-control when you are angry? Do you have clients suddenly leave you for a competitor with no explanation and they avoid your attempts to learn why they left? Does your presence in a tense situation create more tension or relieve the tension?

Here is a good resource if you are interested in learning more about EQ and soft skills development: https://www.mindtools.com/pages/article/newCDV_59.htm[9]

Challenge

Do some research on Emotional Intelligence. Find some free inventories that will help you assess your EQ. Encourage some colleagues to assess their EQ with you and have a few discussions regarding what you discover. In the context of a strong and loyal friendship, ask your friend how they would rate your EQ.

Lesson 16: Power Made Perfect in Weakness

There is a verse in the Bible that says, "My grace is sufficient for you, for my power is made perfect in weakness" (2 Corinthians 12:9). While there is a spiritual context for this truth, I believe the truth of power coming from weakness is also wisdom for our lives. It is true that God has a knack for doing big things, grand things, in very small packages, even weak objects. Jesus fed thousands from one boy's sack lunch. So, what does this have to do with marketing professional services?

I have heard many design professionals in the engineering profession simply dismiss themselves from being good at marketing and business development. This is because most design professionals see themselves as weak in the primary skills of good marketing. They see marketing as requiring soft skills they do not have. Sometimes, they are good at it, but simply do not enjoy it. Time spent flattering clients, schmoozing at a networking event, or entertaining on the golf course is not how they wish to spend their time. Therefore, they simply chalk it up to weakness and excuse themselves from marketing.

But the wisdom of Scripture and promise of God is to demonstrate His power, specifically in your weaknesses. The very skills and personality traits you dismiss as weak, and consequently, never exercise, are the very weaknesses in which God wishes to demonstrate power. For example, by personality and nature, I am not well-organized. I tend to be forgetful and distracted. However, many years ago, I committed to doing better and submitted this weakness to God, asking for help and practicing better organization skills. Now, God has demonstrated His power in me, making me well-organized.

I encourage you to exercise skills that are naturally weak in you. Ask God for help. His power can be made perfect in your weakness.

Another way of examining this same truth is to think of every weakness as a two-sided coin. It is not unusual for people to discover that some of their greatest weaknesses are actually great strengths in disguise. One of my weaknesses (other than being naturally disorganized), is to jump in to make recommendations or suggestions when I should be quiet and listen. This is obnoxious and tends to shut down others who take more time to think things through before speaking up. While I have worked on this weakness and tried to keep my mouth shut in a group and let others speak first, there are situations when speaking up early is helpful to the group leader. Because I am comfortable speaking up, I try to recognize each situation and behave in a manner that is best for the group.

Challenge

What are some of your persistent weaknesses? List out three to five weaknesses and challenge yourself to think about what could be on the other side of that weakness coin. How could you yield to God's desire and power to create strength in these weaknesses?

Lesson 17: These Six Mistakes Can Undermine Your Leadership

John Hall, Co-Founder and President, Calendar.com, suggests six common mistakes leaders make. If you become more aware of these common mistakes, you stand a better chance of noticing and correcting them.

1. Not realizing the importance of emotional intelligence.
2. Inadequately delegating work.
3. Failing to give and receive feedback.
4. Feeling unfocused and uninspired.
5. Not leading by example.
6. Saying you don't have time.

John gives a more thorough explanation of each of the mistakes and what you can do to correct them in this article at Inc.com.[10]

Before you dive more deeply into these six common leadership mistakes, consider yourself a leader. You may be tempted to review this list and think of how people in leadership have flubbed it up. I want you to think of yourself and your areas of leadership and how you may be making some of these mistakes. If I were to guess, those in marketing leadership roles probably struggle with not delegating work tasks, feeling unfocused and uninspired, and complaining that they don't have time. I am not a prophet and I do not have a secret line listening in on your daily work routine. I am a marketing leader and have fallen prey to these mistakes myself. As the ancient Greeks say, "Know thyself."

Challenge

I have already hinted at the challenge of this lesson. Rather than picking apart your leadership, be introspective and receive your mantle of leadership. Consider these six common leadership mistakes and start taking actions to mitigate them. I firmly believe that those who do the work of introspection and create new habits will not only be leaders but will authentically impact their circles of influence for the better. When you consider the positive side of these six mistakes you get the following:

- Valuing the importance of emotional intelligence
- Delegating work appropriately
- Giving and receiving feedback
- Staying focused and inspired
- Leading by a good example
- Making time for others

Lesson 18: Thought Leadership

"Thought Leadership Marketing provides insight into the talents and knowledge base of your organization and takes many forms" (Butcher, Scott D., FSMPS, CPSM, *Marketing 2022: A Survey Exploring Current and Future A/E/C Marketing Practices*).[11]

Because of the proliferation of the internet, the opportunities to get marketing messages in front of clients and prospects at a low cost have exploded. Utilizing websites, social media platforms, and email, marketers can now present their company's stories and messages easier than ever. But as you have experienced, most of these stories and messages disappear in a vast sea of chaotic noise and are ignored!

However, there is one type of message that is not being ignored. Thought leadership messages and stories are both desired and needed by A/E/C clients. Thought leadership marketing is the creation of content that is unique to a professional's expertise and professional achievement. This content can be communicated by writing blogs, whitepapers, or articles. It can be communicated through video production or a webinar broadcast. Design professionals can publish how-to and best practice guides relative to their proficiency. And all this content can be hosted on the company's website, posted on social media channels, and delivered in emails.

Why does thought leadership marketing work in a sea of other digital marketing noise? Because good thought leadership content gives something of value a client can use and is given for free. Valuable content that helps me today rises to the surface and becomes important over-and-above other marketing messages simply asking me to buy something. It also works because it positions the author as an expert who can be trusted. So, when a prospect or client needs engineering services, they will more likely think of someone who has already helped them and is providing value free of charge.

It is best practice to not only push out thought leadership content as general marketing messages but to also be targeted in your messaging. For example, if you have a subject matter expert (SME) who wrote a blog post about a specific construction technique for large diameter sewer line installation, post the link on your social media channels (general), but also have that SME send a direct email to several clients and prospects who have large diameter sewer lines.

It is also best practice to utilize the same content in many formats. If the SME's blog post received great reviews and generated business, you may consider producing a short video relaying the same content. Submit the content for trade journal publication or a presentation at the right conference. In other words, get the most mileage you can from your best content!

Challenge

Ask some of your seasoned design professionals to sit with you and talk about their careers. What were their favorite projects? What is the most significant design challenge they've faced? What is the craziest thing they've seen on the job? As you interview, you will discover valuable content unique to these pros. Ask their permission to record your conversation so you can mine valuable content afterwards. Offer to ghostwrite a blog post based on the stories they share. If they enjoy the conversation and appreciate your writing, ask them to consider telling the story in front of a camera and produce video content.

Lesson 19: Thought Leadership and LinkedIn

One of the best platforms for creating and promoting good thought leadership content is LinkedIn. Unlike other social media platforms, LinkedIn is dedicated to business relationships and the promotion of business networking. Therefore, LinkedIn users are expecting to see and consume valuable content for their business and professional development. Consider the impact of LinkedIn.[12]

- 150 million users in the United States
- 40% of users access LinkedIn daily
- 44% of LinkedIn users take home more than $75,000 annually
- For Business-to-Business (B2B) marketers, 80% of their social media leads come from LinkedIn
- Using a professional photo on your page will get 14 Xs more views than other types of profile photos or no photo at all.
- List at least five relevant skills on your profile to increase generating a relevant business contact by 31 Xs.
- Only about 1% of users share content regularly. That means your content does not get lost in a vast digital sea.

- LinkedIn drives more traffic to B2B blogs and websites than any other social media platform.
- Including a photo, graphic, or short video on a post increases the comment rate by 98%

I wrote this Monday Marketing Tip on May 4, 2020. Nearly six months later, I took my advice and started utilizing LinkedIn for both my personal thought leadership and my company's thought leadership and promotion. I made our company LinkedIn page a priority in late July 2020. In three months, we accomplished the following:

- o Increased followers 21%, from 332 to 418.
- o We have posted 30 times, an average of 2.5 posts per week.
- o Average organic impressions are 107, with organic average engagement at 6%.

While these numbers didn't blow anyone away, we felt good about the start. This gave us a baseline of data from which to improve.

Challenge

If you are not utilizing LinkedIn to find and nurture business relationships you are significantly behind the curve. Get going on both your profile and the company page! Start interacting regularly on LinkedIn and find ways to get valuable thought leadership content in front of your LinkedIn community.

Lesson 20: Earn the Role of Trusted Advisor

The following advice is adapted from the Marketer article, "How to Earn the Role of Trusted Advisor," written by Michael Buell, FSMPS, Assoc. DBIA.[13]

As a professional engineer and technical expert, your primary task is planning and designing infrastructure that society needs to function efficiently and safely. You work for a firm that must compete with other firms to earn or win business. One of the best ways to entrench a client with you and your firm is to move from being an engineer among many to a trusted advisor. The trusted advisor is always the one called first and most when a client has a need.

An engaging personality is powerful. A strong presence in the room is powerful. Being confident, enlightening, or inspiring is powerful. But the one who earns the trust of a client is the most critical virtue in long-term and fruitful client relationships.

The key to becoming the trusted advisor is genuineness. The moment your interactions become 'agenda-driven' is the moment the client feels you have become entitled. Genuineness comes from the desire to help, even if that help comes from somewhere other than you or your firm. If another professional or competing firm has a better solution to your client's problem, genuineness means advising the client to hire that person or firm. Just remember this phrase, "Help, Don't Sell!" Stay focused on the client's needs.

My firm had recently won our first assignment from a new client. The client is a mid-sized municipality in the Midwest who needed help modeling and managing their water system data. The city's leadership had a taste for growth and had implemented several initiatives to both prepare for and spur the desired growth. They wanted their water system to be ready to accommodate growth.

After several months serving this need, we were asked to submit our qualifications to widen a 1.5 mile stretch of two-lane road to a three-lane road. We reviewed the scope of work and determined that while we were technically capable we also knew our workload was too heavy, which would severely limit our ability to produce a project on time. Rather than competing for the project, we decided to gracefully decline. But I went one step further. I called the Public Works Director and explained our decision and recommended who I thought the top two competitors were for this project.

He was stunned. "Why are you recommending your competitors? No one ever does this."

I replied, "If we are your best option we will tell you that. If someone else is a better option, we will tell you that. We are more interested in our long-term relationship with you than trying to win all your work."

That single conversation with a new client solidified our role. We are trusted advisors, not salesmen. You can trust our judgment and advice because we tell you what is best for *you*, not what gets us the most work.

Challenge

What can you do to train and assist your seller-doers and business developers to think more like trusted advisors and less like salesmen? When you make no-go decisions, always make sure you or someone representing your firm is following up with an explanation. If you are being genuine, let them know who you think would do a good job for them if that someone is available and competing.

Lesson 21: 7 Leadership Thinking Traps

There are likely areas of thinking in which you are getting stuck. As a leader, you are responsible for your performance and the performance of your teammates. Consider these seven leadership thinking traps and their solutions (adapted from Kim Ades' article, "Overcoming Seven Leadership Thinking Traps").[14]

1. **Tunnel Vision:** Do you simply cross off items on your 'to-do list' without ever thinking about strategy, goal setting, vision casting, or professional development? You and your team need thinking space to consider more than just your day-to-day tasks.

Solution: Journaling is a powerful tool to help you focus, manage emotions, and keep sight of the future. Journaling increases problem-solving and gets your mind out of tunnel vision mode.

2. **Isolation:** Do you shoulder the burden of success on your own? Do you prefer to keep most project tasks and are reluctant to hand over responsibilities to your team? Do you feel no one can do the job as well as you? You've isolated yourself and become easily overwhelmed.

Solution: Actively seek out strong team members and trust them with important project tasks. Utilize experts outside of your organization for support. Consider temporarily hiring a life coach to help you learn to trust and share your work.

3. **Image Management:** Do you find that you deflect blame when things go wrong? Is it difficult for you to take responsibility and apologize? Do you fear public fallout and personal failure? Being very successful can lead to unhealthy behaviors attempting to uphold a successful image.

Solution: Learn that admitting mistakes and an appropriate apology make you more human, and therefore, more approachable. Utilize trusted internal and external advisors to help you navigate the recovery of a mistake or poor decision.

4. **Poor Decision-Making:** During fast-paced or high-pressure seasons, it is easy to make quick decisions that don't feel right. Do you find that you ignore your instincts

and make poor decisions in the interest of 'getting things done?' Do you find that a series of poor decisions have led you into a situation that becomes difficult or impossible to back out of?

Solution: Learn to make decisions that align with your values, morals, and priorities, even if it may not be efficient now. Hold in high regard the values of your company. Hold yourself accountable for personal ethics.

5. **Complacency:** When things are running smoothly, it is easy to work in a rut and find yourself in a routine that leads to complacency. Have you lost your drive to challenge the status quo? Have you stopped learning and investing in your professional development?

Solution: To be a good leader you must look out for opportunities to change, improve, and grow. When you become complacent, so does your team. The only solution is to either retire or start taking risks, make bold decisions, and challenge yourself.

6. **Shortsightedness:** Do you find that you only think about what is in front of you for the day and fail to look into the future? You may be good at fighting today's fires, but you and your team are ill-prepared for tomorrow. Do you know what is happening with your clients and their industry for the next five to ten years?

Solution: When solving today's problems, take time to see the long-term effects of today's decisions. Work through problems with an eye on the long-term strategy. Take the time to research and think about your job, your role, and your clients' problems for the next several years.

7. **Fear of Failure:** Do you often play it safe to avoid failure? Do you turn down new ideas or avoid acting because you are afraid of making mistakes? Do you view past mistakes as personal flaws or catastrophes? Fear of

failure keeps many talented professionals stagnant.

Solution – Failure is part of success. Learn how to leverage your failures and turn them into new opportunities. See failure as part of your growth. Do not allow your setbacks to define you, but discover how to bounce back with emotional resilience. Take time to review what went wrong and write down lessons learned.

If you discover thinking traps in your work life, do something about them! It is never too late to grow and become the leader you were created to be.

Challenge

Review these seven thinking traps and do a quick self-assessment. What traps do you fall into? Are there things you could be doing differently to avoid these traps? If you discover that you are in several ruts from which you just cannot escape, think about hiring a life coach. Life coaching is perfect for helping leaders see blind spots and provide objective analysis.

Lesson 22: Lead Yourself

Leaders are taught, not born. Leaders are learners, not naturally talented. Leaders learn from failure, not always successful. To be a good leader, one must want to lead and put in the necessary work. Ford Harding, the author of the bestselling book, *Rain Making: Attract New Clients No Matter What Your Field*,[15] says he discovered several commonalities in all-star business leaders.

• Leaders are highly productive early in their careers. Leaders learned early to develop client relationships and build loyalty. These young professionals found the unpopular project others in the firm did not like and cranked out project after project in unpopular disciplines. This mix of client relationship building and productivity creates marketing savvy few young professionals are willing to develop.

- Leaders take an interest in marketing early in their careers. Leaders find marketing tasks they are either good at or can develop and exercise those tasks to perfection. For some, it may be networking and the ability to build a large and loyal network of professionals who feed them consistent leads. For others, it may be writing excellent marketing content, project photography, presenting subject matter expertise, cross-selling other services, etc.

- Leaders credential themselves and never stop learning. Whatever your field, leaders understand the value of credentialing and specializing. Leaders discover opportunities to both expand and deepen their skills, both technical and business. Formal recognition of your abilities establishes trust and confidence with clients. Great leaders never stop learning or growing in their profession.

- Leaders look for ways to improve their firm's services. Beyond their personal brand and ability to produce, leaders have a keen eye for continual improvement. Leaders find ways to save money, create efficiencies, and improve the business performance of their firms. This happens primarily because leaders find ways to make and keep clients happy.

- Leaders eventually become specialists. Rather than generalizing, doing different projects with different clients in different markets, leaders hone in on one or two areas of specialty and become experts with deep knowledge and experience. This depth creates a bench of steady clients and a stellar reputation within the leader's given market.

Challenge

My challenge to you is this: Make yourself a good leader. Do not settle for letting your career come to you, but create the career you want. Be productive, learn to market, credential, improve your company, and specialize.

Lesson 23: Make Them Want What You Do

If you look at the architecture and engineering business (notice I didn't say 'A/E/C' because I don't think 'construction' is part of the same 'industry'), I think we can all agree that clients of firms in this business generally hire you because they need your services. They don't necessarily want those services, but they need them.

Clients need A/E firms so they can get their property rezoned, so they can get building permits, so they can get competitive bids from contractors to build something, and much more. I never fully appreciated this fact until I became a developer about 15 years ago. Even though we had in-house design, we still needed structural engineers to stamp retaining walls, civil engineers to do drainage plans, geotechnical engineers to give soils data to the structural engineers, land surveyors to do topographical surveys for the civil engineers, and registered architects to stamp tenant improvement plans in commercial buildings we owned. All necessary stuff.

As a developer I was often guilty of all the same sins I complained about in developer clients when I was on the other side of the fence inside an A/E firm selling services. Price was a major consideration. Shortly after price came reliability. Would the A/E firm get done what we needed done? Time is money. And as far as architectural services for building design were concerned, my number one criteria (after price) was if the architecture firm would do what I wanted them to do, or if there would be a battle because they wanted to do what *they* wanted to do.

All of this is fine—it's great to be needed—but it's not

really where you want to be. The position you should really seek to attain is to be *wanted*; wanted because you have something no one else has or no one else can do as well as you do. The reason this is important is because it takes the focus off price.

If you want to be wanted versus just a necessary evil competing with other firms on price, here are some things you need to do:

- **Have something unique to offer.** This is so important and fundamental. You cannot do everything the same way everyone else does and create the same kinds of products everyone else does and then expect to be wanted. You have to do something unique and better. That takes a push for constant improvement and innovation in both your process and your outputs. Our business works against 'new' and 'innovative.' There's risk associated with that. It may not work. It may cost more to design or take longer to build because the contractors aren't familiar with it. But that is a risk you may need to take to create real value for your clients that their other providers can't or won't do.

- **Build a lot of awareness of your firm and your work through PR.** I'm talking about being in the media constantly. Being in the mainstream media is always better than the industry-specialized media, when the public at large knows who you are and what you do. Make your firm principals into public figures that people know (or want to know). Make your people 'people' who clients want to do business with because they think they will learn something from you. Make your people 'people' who clients want to hang out with because they are interesting and smart and funny. You can do that but you won't do it with just another boring project description. Focus on the people. It takes a relentless and consistent effort to come up with 'man bites dog' kinds of press versus 'dog bites man' kinds of stuff.

- **Get people talking about you.** Again, this will only come from your real effort to do something new and better, and from selling the personalities you have leading your firm and your projects. Taking the safe and expedient route every time will not accomplish this goal. Of course, not everyone will like you or your work when you do this. That's okay. This is a real big hurdle to overcome for most people in this business who are trying to please everyone and never offend anyone. And yes, taste is subjective.

- **Have some big successes you can point to.** Project cases—what the problem or opportunity was, what you did for your clients, and how that translated into benefits for them—are at the heart of selling successes. I find most firms' project descriptions do not accomplish this. They instead list facts about the project but little of the back story on how the project developed and even less about what happened after it was built. Not the way to really create desire for what you do. You want clients reading these cases and saying, "Wow – *these* are the people we should be working with!" I won't say it is easy to develop good cases for firms in this business. I'm not sure why that is the case, but it is usually a battle to get these done properly.

- **Be selective about the clients you work for.** Not all clients will enhance your reputation. You have to be willing to say 'no.' The only way I know how to accomplish this is to have more clients who want you than you can serve. If you cannot drive demand beyond your ability to supply it, you will take work from clients you should not be taking. Make them want you by being hard to get. Being too easy doesn't necessarily make them want you. We all want what we cannot have.

- **Be willing to walk away from anyone who abuses you in any way.** This is so important because the collective morale of everyone in your business depends in large part on you and what kind of behaviors you will tolerate from your clients. If you make it absolutely clear that no price is high enough to subject yourself and your people to abuse, you make your firm more desirable to work with for (good) clients.

Creating 'want' versus 'need' may seem counterintuitive. Being in a business that clients need is usually enough. But the question is do they need *your* firm, or just *a* firm? You should want to achieve the former versus the latter. And that's going to take doing things differently for most firms in the A/E business.

Guest writer, Mark Zweig. "Make them want what you do!" The Zweig Letter[16]

Challenge

Mark Zweig has the unique position of having sat on both sides of the fence: a service provider and an owner/developer. His insights in creating a desire for your services are worth spending some extra time to think about and implement. One of the main themes of this lesson is the person of the engineer or architect. Start thinking about selling yourself, not just what you do. Be bold in offering unique or different solutions. Take public relations seriously and create a legitimate PR strategy. Do not try and please everyone, but rather step out to let your ideas be heard. Learn to be a good storyteller. Do not work for everyone, but work for those who value you and value what you do. And fire the clients who are abusing you and sapping your creativity.

Lesson 24: Business Wisdom from Proverbs

Proverbs 27:23–24: "Know the state of your flocks, and put your heart into caring for your herds, for riches don't last forever, and the crown might not be passed to the next generation."

This simple proverb reminds us to pay attention to the state of our business. Knowing the state of our flocks and caring for our herds means several things. Even though this wisdom was written in an agrarian society, the principles are timeless.

1. Our flocks are our projects and service offerings. Some good questions to consider the state of our projects and services include:

   a. Is this project staying on schedule and within budget?

   b. Are we pricing this service offering accurately to make a consistent profit?

   c. Is our client receiving what was expected or are they disappointed in some way?

2. Caring for our herds looks like taking care of both our human capital, our employees, as well as our clients.

   a. Is an employee under my care getting burned out, bored with their assignments, developing lazy work habits? What can I do to nurture a healthy employee?

   b. Is an employee under my care in the right position? Are we making the most of their talents and abilities?

   c. Am I working for clients who enjoy and appreciate what I do for them or am I stuck with clients who complain and take me for granted?

   d. What clients do I wish I could work for and how can I win them over to hire us?

Wealth does not last forever. While our companies may be blessed this year, we cannot take it for granted that this will always be the case. Biblical wisdom recommends that we pay attention to the state of our business now and care for what we have. We are also wise to invest our time and energy in the next generation of leadership so they are also prepared to carry the business forward in growth and prosperity!

Challenge

The challenge for this lesson is in the already asked questions. If you want to know the state of your business these questions can be asked and answered. If you have authority over a business unit or department, the same questions can be asked of your area of responsibility.

Lesson 25: Who Determines Your Success

The great leadership speaker and expert, John Maxwell said, "Those closest to you determine your level of success."

He shared several questions to help us determine our inner circle, those on our team with whom we share most of our time and energy. It is this small group of team members who will determine our level of success. This is personal success, but also impacts our company's success.

- Do they live out good values?

What are your values? You want to surround yourself with people who share your most treasured and prioritized values. These include values such as honesty, trustworthiness, patience, detail-oriented, organized, self-motivated, etc. You do not have to have identical values, but the highest priority values should align on a team.

- Do they have a high influence on others?

Influence is the ability to affect the actions, behaviors,

and opinions of others. Great team members demonstrate influence. They are the kind of people others want to work for and be around. High influence people inspire and motivate by word and deed. What they say and what they do are aligned.

- Do they have gifts that complement the team?

If everyone on the team is highly gifted at quality review with an eye for details, but no one on the team is gifted at initiative, you have a problem. No one will ever get started so there will be nothing to review. Find people with complementary gifts, not people just like you.

- Can they lead and equip others?

Leading others includes equipping them to do what is asked. Equipping can include teaching, technology, tools, or all three. You want to surround yourself with others who can pass on their talents and skills. Good leadership includes replacing yourself with others who do it better than you.

- Are they a good fit for the inner circle?

This is a gut-level judgment. It is an intangible quality that is either present or absent. After spending a little time with someone, you can use your intuition to determine if you believe you will work well together. Being a good fit is about good collaboration not only with you but with others on the team.

- Can they produce excellent results?

At the end of the day, good team members produce. They get the job done and do it well. To achieve success, everyone pulls weight. Pulling weight means pulling in the same direction and everyone participates. Do not keep people in your inner circle who weigh more than they can carry.

- Do they value people and serve them?

Every business is a people business. No matter the technical expertise, what you do directly impacts people. Even if you are technically-minded and prefer to work with things rather than people, the things you work with ultimately serve people. Surround yourself with team members who understand their everyday work is about people and serving them well!

Challenge

Audit your inner circle. Who do you spend most of your time and energy with at work? Who makes up your primary team? Run through these questions and assess the quality of your inner circle. If you discover there is some incongruence, do you have the ability and authority to change the team? If you do, then consider what steps you need to take to improve the quality of your inner circle. If you do not have the authority to change your team, use these questions as a springboard to have conversations with your team about becoming more congruent.

Bonus: If you have no control or authority over your team at work, find some colleagues from other teams or other non-competing companies and create your own inner circle. Carve out regular time to invest in these people and let them invest in you. For many years, I was a marketing department of one at a small engineering firm. I created an inner circle of colleagues from non-competing companies who shared similar job descriptions as mine. We encouraged each other's success, which also benefitted each of our companies.

Chapter 3 – Business Development

Lesson 26: Making Long-Term Investment

Zweig Group CEO Chad Clinehens wrote a very nice article[17] regarding some tips for taking a long-term investment approach in our A/E/C business. Here are a few highlights:

- **Focus on client experience**. Most firms are doing worse at client experience. Zweig is observing declining satisfaction scores, especially in the areas of accessibility and responsiveness. Firms are saying, "We are just too busy."

- **High workloads are shifting focus to putting out fires rather than proactively servicing clients**. Asking clients to provide feedback and not doing anything with the information is worse than never asking at all. Be careful that your flexible work practices do not erode the client experience.

- **Spend more on marketing and business development**. Over the last three years, Zweig Group has seen a declining investment in marketing and BD activity. In a highly competitive market, now is the time to invest more in marketing and BD resources to build a backlog and brand preference. It is critical to act while the economy is good. There will come a day when your clients have fewer dollars to spend. Position yourself now so they spend those dollars with you.

- **Commit to continuous learning firm wide**. The number one challenge firms face is recruiting and retention. The number one benefit identified and highly valued by employees of A/E/C firms for the past two years is training and development.

- **Make strategic planning a yearly activity**. The opportunity for you to make your firm strong now when times are good will greatly improve your resilience in future turbulent economic times. Firms with strategic plans are 12% more profitable and enjoy stronger recruiting abilities.

Zweig Group is dedicated to recommending best practices based on solid research and data. These investments in client experience, responsiveness, marketing and business development, training, and strategic planning will produce positive results. The clients say so and the data proves it.

Challenge

Whatever your position of influence or decision-making within your firm, commit to staying focused on these areas of investment. Do not allow the everyday fires and distractions to keep you from a planned and strategic investment into the parts of your business that make the biggest impact.

Lesson 27: Business Development in 11 Words

"Yes, I know it's not Monday ... it's Tuesday! But here's your weekly dose of marketing medicine anyway." (That is how I began this email later in the week. I decided to keep it in this book because it illustrates something of value: humor. Don't get so bogged down in the minutia of the day-to-day that you miss opportunities for humor.)

This marketing tip was adapted from Michael Buell's Marketer article, "The Entire BD Process in 11 Words."[18] The process of business development, especially as it relates to engineering services is quite simple. Here is a short excerpt from the article.

> *"Sales is a result–business development is the process! Yes, we're trying to generate sales, but with professional services that should be considered the preferred culmination of effective and timely marketing and business development efforts."*

It is a good reminder to recognize that a sale happens after multiple business development tasks and marketing efforts have been accomplished. Michael Buell offers the following 11 words condensing the BD process: Identify, Engage, Listen, Understand, Respond, Inform, Pursue, Affirm, Win, Fortify, Cultivate.

Identify whether a prospective client is a good fit for your firm.

Engage the prospect. This may be a requested meeting, a shared networking event or conference, a phone call, or email.

Listen. Now that you are engaged with a prospect, be prepared with great questions, make them comfortable to talk, and listen.

Understand their goals, interests, ideas, likes, and dislikes. Get to know them and their organization.

Respond to the prospect's requests and needs. Be quick in your responses and be helpful.

Inform your prospects of industry trends, funding opportunities, best practices, or anything else they may find useful and beneficial to their job.

Pursue opportunities for project tasks. Only after identifying, engaging, listening, understanding, responding, and informing do you now ask for work and pursue it!

Affirm everything you have learned about the prospect in previous stages and incorporate it into your pursuit of work.

Win the work!

Fortify your new client relationship with planned client experience touches. This can be done through a mix of client surveying, debriefing, entertainment, and a rock-solid work product.

Cultivate the initial steps by continuing to engage, listen, understand, respond, inform, and pursue. Create great client experiences with every project, solidifying your commitment, and the client's loyalty.

Challenge

Look at your prospect list as it is right now. Take your top several prospects and determine where you are in the business development process. Have you skipped over any critical phases? Are you following the process? Commit yourself to faithfully aligning your BD activities with these 11 phases and measure the results.

Lesson 28: Business Development is Served

Have you ever wondered why business developers go out to eat all the time? It seems that BD people are always looking to go out for lunch with someone and it is usually a client, a prospect, or someone who can get us to a client or prospect. These lunches are purposeful. If they are well-planned and executed, business lunches can provide a treasure of intelligence and insight leading to more work.

Here are some tips for a great business development lunch. If you plan ahead and execute your plan, you can help gain more work for your company.

Tip #1: Show up 10-15 minutes earlier than scheduled. You don't want your client waiting on you.

This may be difficult because there's always one more email to read or one more piece of information to circulate before you get out of the office. And of course, several people are wanting your time and will ask for it as you are trying to walk out the door. Do whatever you must, but get yourself to the restaurant early so you are there to greet your guest when he or she arrives. Being early and greeting your guests is hospitable and shows you are there exclusively for them.

Tip #2: Go prepared with knowledge of the client's organization (operations, history, current needs, and challenges).

Like any good project execution, you must have a well-researched plan. Creating a successful business development lunch also requires that you know who you are visiting, why you are visiting them, and how they relate to their organization. Have some general knowledge of their business, their industry, and typical issues they may have. If you cannot discover very much, then the business lunch is a perfect time to ask, which leads directly to Tip #3.

Tip #3: Ask questions about the client organization.

Be prepared to ask open-ended questions. What are your biggest concerns, obstacles, issues? Where do you hope to be in five to ten years? What makes your company better than competitors? Start with big, over-arching questions before asking specific 'engineering-related' questions. Ask questions like you are on a date, not an FBI interrogator. A good date listens and is genuinely interested in you. That is how you want your questions to land.

Tip #4: Show genuine interest in everything, even if it doesn't apply to your services.

If they want to talk about their pets, their car, their kids, or whatever, just listen and show interest. Small talk is a way for the client to get used to you, examine, and trust you. It is okay if you spend more time talking about nothing, as long as it is building trust and a genuine connection. Once you feel the connection is good, ease into more business-related topics.

Tip #5: Make sure your server knows early in the meal that you will be picking up the tab.

Get this task out of the way early. I prefer to let the server know as we are initially being seated that I will be paying the bill for the meal. If you are ordering at a counter, simply ask your guest to order first and you will pick up the bill. This only gets awkward when people make it awkward. Smile, be courteous, and simply make it natural.

On occasion, you may be eating with a government employee who cannot let you pay for their meal. You must accommodate the rules of their employer, so simply say you understand and let them pay for their meal.

Tip #6: Turn off your phone or at least put it on silent and *do not check it*! Only take a phone call if you think it is an emergency.

Everyone agrees with good phone etiquette but I rarely view people practicing it. This is serious and can damage your best efforts if you violate respectful phone manners. If it is too tempting to respond to the vibrations, then turn it off. Do whatever is necessary to make sure you are not answering or checking your phone during your lunch meeting. Checking your phone or answering a call says to your guest, "I have someone or something more important than you right now." That is not the message you want to send.

I recall going to lunch with a business developer for an industry-related firm with whom my firm occasionally partnered. I had initiated the meeting and he recommended a great lunch spot. When I arrived, he was already present and waiting. We were seated and he informed our waiter he would be taking the ticket. Then he did something remarkable and memorable. He took out his mobile phone and shut it off. He literally said, "You and this meal are the most important things for the next hour, so you have my undivided attention." I, of course, had to oblige and turned off my phone as well. It was refreshing and warm to stay engaged in conversation with a colleague and friend throughout a meal with no phone interruptions and no chance for one.

Tip #7: Do not sell!

Do not confuse business development with selling. You are not out to lunch to sell anything. You are out to lunch to build a relationship with someone who may or may not need your services. You are there to represent your company and discover if the person with whom you are dining perceives value in knowing you. Business is people and it is personal. If someone feels like a means to your ultimate end, they will feel used and disconnected. You want them to leave lunch feeling heard, understood, and valued.

Make a purposeful plan and recognize you are doing a job. Your job is to learn and understand more about your client or prospect and translate that knowledge into opportunities to solve their problems. Having lunch together is a social event with the expectation to enjoy each other's company. It may take a couple of lunches before the relational trust is built, so be patient and follow these seven tips to ensure business development success.

Challenge

Before your next BD lunch, review these tips. If you do nothing else right, get one thing right: *turn off your phone!* This is not a pet peeve. I am doing you a tremendous favor. You will differentiate yourself from nearly every competitor with the simple step of turning off your phone. You will be tempted to argue the need to be available. I will argue that as soon as you so much as look at your phone in front of a client or prospect you have communicated that whatever you are looking at or whomever you are talking with on your phone is more important than they are.

Lesson 29: Managing Client Relationships: 7 Tips

Once you have secured a client, the next phase of business development is to maintain your client relationship. Indeed, the cost of gaining a new client is significantly higher than retaining an existing client. Therefore, whatever you can do to improve your client management is worth your time. (Adapted from Hubspot.com, author Nathan Resnick)[19]

1. Involve your client in goal-setting.

    Rather than viewing your job as completing projects and tasks, take a step back and see the 'big picture.' What is your client trying to accomplish? The best way to discover the answer is to sit down with your client and discuss their business goals. Help them think through their goals, offering encouragement and advice. Take part in the client's goal-setting process. This positions you as a partner in their business, not just a vendor providing a service.

2. Answer questions before they are asked.

    This doesn't mean you can't answer your client's questions. It does mean you should be proactive in your communication. In other words, you should be the one to take initiative. I wrote a tip in Chapter 4, Lesson 42 about being 'Responsive' to your clients. That tip has to do with keeping clients well-informed. This is the same thing. Well-informed clients get answers to questions they didn't know they had.

3. Put the onus back on your client, when necessary.

    There are certain pieces of critical data and information that only your client knows. If you want to do a good job on your next project, set up systems that make it easy for your client to deliver that critical data. Plan ahead and ask for the data as soon as possible. Utilize PDF forms or common cloud servers (Google Drive or Dropbox) to make data sharing easy.

4. Address client needs before they know they exist.

Clients do not always know what they need. This may be the primary reason they are hiring you. Put yourself in your client's shoes and understand the problem from their perspective. Address your recommended solutions from their perspective. This is an opportunity for you to teach your client and make them smarter. Just like answering questions before they are asked, this takes initiative.

5. Use the old and dated technology of a phone call.

Even though emails are more convenient, they are not always the best communication tool when solving a problem. Pick up the phone and call when you know there needs to be some discussion and understanding in solving the client's problem. Phone calls are also more personal and effective in hearing the tone and pace of the message. You can always follow up a phone call with an email summary that clarifies the communication and documents any decisions made.

6. Don't be petty, condescending, or difficult.

Your client may be unpleasant, rude, and difficult, but that never should permit you to be the same. When engaged in a business relationship, be on your best behavior. Do not ignore their calls or emails. Do not be condescending in your tone or attitude. Do not treat their business or project as trivial. Treat clients with respect, even if it is underserving. You can always fire the client after a project closeout if it is unbearable.

7. Be transparent, even when it doesn't look good.

Despite your best efforts, you will make mistakes. Dishonesty is much worse than simply admitting a mistake and doing what you can to correct it. Do not waste time worrying about what your client may say or do and delay being transparent. Ask for wisdom from seasoned engineers and then take your lumps. It is not unusual for a client's loyalty to increase after you make a mistake if you have taken responsibility and done everything you can to correct it.

Challenge

These tips are simply reinforcing common social graces. An attitude of courtesy and kindness will make these tips common sense. Following the Golden Rule to do for others what you would like done for you is also advice worth following. Assess your attitude toward clients, especially more difficult clients. Are you empathizing well? Are you considering their pressures and challenges?

Lesson 30: High-Level Relationships

As an engineering consultant, you are frequently interacting with high-level relationships in your client's organization. For example, you may find that you are interacting with a city manager, utility general manager, attorney, or similar high-level leader. These leaders have high demands on their time and attention. They are typically swamped with requests and other consultants vying for their attention.

Like any good relationship, trust is the bedrock of a valuable relationship. In business, trust means you are not wasting the leader's time. It means you are authentic and exercise wisdom. Here are a few tips for maintaining valuable interactions with high-level relationships and building trust.

- **Follow Through.** Do what you say you will do. This sounds simple, but it is too easy for you to get busy and forget promises or commitments. If you say you will do something, you better have a reliable practice of reminding yourself to follow through! Use your calendar and phone reminders.

- **Give Before You Receive.** What can you do to help this high-level leader in the moment? Do they need a listening ear? Do they need a referral? Do they need a problem solved? Look to give them something of value rather than asking them for work.

- **Be Authentic.** Yes, you are an expert. You may not be the expert they need. Be real with yourself and your capabilities. Be willing to help them find the right expert to solve their problem. When you are the right answer to their problem, great! Being authentic also means exercising humility and simply being yourself.

These are very simple tips for maintaining a successful and trustworthy high-level relationship. These can also be followed when trying to establish a new relationship with a high-level leader. Good business development practice dictates that rather than starting a relationship by asking for something, especially their time, offer something you know is valuable. Send an industry article, introduce them to another expert you know they need, be brief and direct in your communications.

Challenge

High-level relationships are both rewarding and challenging. It is hard to get quality time with a high-level leader. As much as you may like small talk, high-level leaders rarely enjoy small talk in a business setting. Challenge yourself to be direct and respectful. Get in, get to the point, and get out. High-level leaders typically know the cost of doing good business, so once you are in, your projects should be profitable.

Lesson 31: What is the Value of a CRM?

CRM is an acronym for Client/Customer Relationship Management. Maximum CRM utilization in commercial retail companies always collects data on customers and uses that data to analyze, profile, and sell to the customer. Every piece of data that can be collected, organized, and analyzed to create an advantage for a sale is used.

However, for professional services, CRM behaves differently. Business to business (B2B) selling of professional services requires different data and a different approach to sales. The goals of an effective CRM for professional services are:

- **Loyalty-building objectives rather than short sell objectives.** While the business to customer (B2C) company is interested in short selling and volume of sales for profit, B2B professional services are more profitable with loyal client relationships that order repeat work. Therefore, CRM is focused on building client loyalty. Data that supports loyalty building includes anything that helps the service provider better understand the client's world, their pain, frustration, obstacles, challenges, etc.

- **Tracking and analyzing trends.** By collecting good data in a CRM, the B2B practitioner can view trends over time which help forecast market conditions and better position services for the client. The best predictor of the future is what has happened in the past.

- **Consistency in relationship nurturing.** When was the last time I had a meal with that client? Was that 2014 or 2015 when we golfed at that conference together? Did we perform that study in '08 or was it earlier than that? Everyone in the firm is better knowing the answers to these questions or at least being able to find them quickly. Relationship nurturing is making sure we are taking care of clients, especially when they do not have any work going with us. An effectively utilized CRM stores this data and provides a relationship history.

- **Automate redundant data for greater efficiency.** In marketing our services, we often are using redundant data in qualifications and proposals. When that data is organized and easily retrievable, it serves to produce greater efficiency and accuracy. Most CRM systems are capable of collating and retrieving that data effectively.

- **Increase focus on desirable clients and projects.** The better a CRM system is utilized, the better analysis of which clients and projects are most profitable and enjoyable for the company. One of the best uses of a CRM is helping companies realize which clients and projects are costing more than they are worth. Over time, seeing these trends help shape better business development and more profitability.

- **Legacy for future employees.** One of the greatest advantages to a well-run CRM is the legacy created for future leaders and employees. What advantages could you enjoy if you had access to twenty or thirty years of client relationship data? How could you better serve your present clients if you could read and analyze the history of your firm's relationships for several decades?

My firm implemented an industry-specific CRM in 2019. While we are still building our database of client information and learning how best to utilize this tool, we have already experienced significant benefits. We are saying yes to the right project opportunities and more no's to the wrong opportunities. We are finding reliable data quicker making proposal production more efficient. We are just starting to see trends for better forecasting. In short, CRM use is improving our business and will continue to do so with greater pace.

As of this writing we are enjoying a 50% hit rate by count of proposals and 44% hit rate by volume of revenue for the civil division. As far as I can research, my 66-year-old company has never had this level of hit rate. I firmly believe the utilization of our CRM has had a lot to do with this change.

Challenge

You do not have to break your budget to utilize a robust CRM system. There are available CRMs that will do a fine job without you spending tens of thousands of dollars. I challenge you to do your research and find what best fits your company and your goals. Once researched, share your research with firm leaders and make a recommendation on what to purchase.

If you are already employing a CRM, perform an audit of your data and how you are using your system. Find efficiencies in reporting. Sign up for a webinar with the CRM customer support or education division. Make the most of what you already have!

Lesson 32: Email Marketing & Business Development

Some may think email marketing is for the business-to-consumer markets only and does not belong in sophisticated business-to-business markets. I agree that no one in our target industries will make a purchasing decision based on a clever email marketing campaign. For engineering services, purchasing decisions are made based on trust. And you cannot build trust with email campaigns, can you?

Email messages alone will never work in getting a prospective client to hire you. However, email messages can play a significant role in the complex sales cycle leading to a purchasing decision. If done right, a well-timed and well-written email message can help move a prospect closer to hiring you. However, a poorly-timed and poorly-written email message will do the opposite and push them away. So how do you craft a well-timed and well-written email?

Here are a few tips for writing effective emails that will get read and responded to.

o   Keep it brief, very brief!

Email needs to be read quickly. You know this because when you open an unsolicited email that has more than 100 words, you will either scan it, ignore it, or delete it. Well, so does everyone else. They are too busy to read fluff. So, keep unsolicited emails requesting someone's time very brief; 40–75 words is about right.

o   Be specific.

Get to the point immediately! Make your request within the first or second sentence. Busy professionals appreciate brevity, simplicity, and directness.

o   Have a direct subject line.

Your email may not even get opened if you do not have a direct subject line. Be specific and direct in your subject line. If I am asking for an appointment with someone my subject line typically reads, "Request for Appointment," or "Available Next Week?" Three to five words should be the maximum word count for a subject line.

o   Make connections.

If the receiver of your email has mutual connections with you that are relevant to the subject of your message, mention those connections. Sometimes, it is appropriate to carbon copy (CC) mutual connections, so they know you are leaning on your network relationships for validity. It may even be appropriate to let your mentioned connections know you are reaching out to someone they know and why, before you send the email.

o   Give suggestions and make it easy.

If you are asking for their time or information, make it as easy as possible for them to reply to you. Give them suggested dates/times for meeting. Your brevity and straightforward tone let them know you respect their time and will continue to do so if granted an appointment.

o Always thank them.

Be sure to let them know you appreciate them considering your request. Thank them for their role in serving their organization. This shows respect and lets them know you are aware of their position, authority, and influence.

o Let your message marinate.

If you do not get a response right away, do not hassle them with additional emails too soon. I typically let an email marinate for at least a week before reaching out again. If the receiver is a prospect and my email is an unsolicited 'cold call,' I may wait a month before contacting them again. Most busy professionals appreciate your patience, but also your diligence.

Challenge

Audit the last email you sent to a prospective client. Run through these seven tips and grade yourself on how well you kept to these seven tips. Create a prospect 'cold call' email template that honors these seven tips. Use that template whenever you email a prospect. A sample of my most recent prospective client email is in Appendix A.

Lesson 33: Business Development for Introverts

Business Development (BD) is often perceived as being for the extroverts. After all, so much handshaking, meeting new people, networking in large crowds. It almost sounds like an introvert's nightmare! However, there is much more to effective BD then being a social butterfly.

Here are a few tips for introverts to succeed in BD tasks.

- Before meeting with a prospective or new client, research them on LinkedIn and their company website. Find some things you may have in common, mutual interests, to develop conversation starters.

- Be curious and ask questions. One of the extrovert's weaknesses is naturally talking about themselves or their company. The secret BD weapon of the introvert is your natural curiosity and wish to take the spotlight off yourself.

- If you are attending a networking event, obtain the attendance list in advance. Discover a handful of people with whom you would like to visit and contact them ahead of the event to let them know you look forward to visiting with them.

- Practice good self-care (nutrition, exercise, and sleep) and schedule alone time when attending a conference or longer event. Let yourself recharge.

- An introvert's strength is the ability for deep thought and reflection. However, the wisdom generated from such deep thinking is of no value unless you are willing to share it with others. Challenge yourself to share your thoughts in appropriate settings.

- One of the most significant tasks of a good business developer is nurturing existing client relationships. Check in regularly with current clients and practice asking your curious probing questions with already established relationships.

- Good BD is a marathon, not a sprint. Establish rapport, build credibility, and develop the chemistry and trust needed for a good working relationship. There is no pressure to land a new client after an introductory meeting.

- Be yourself! Genuineness and authenticity sell better than techniques and talent. By the way, this is a good list for extroverts to follow as well.

Adapted from, "Can an Introvert Succeed at BD? (Yes, Here's How)," by Rich Friedman, *Marketer Journal*, October, 2018.[20]

Challenge

If you classify yourself as an introvert and have business development responsibilities, look through this list of tips and choose a couple of them to work on. Based on the tips you choose, set some measurable goals to achieve in the next six months. Place reminders on your calendar or notifications on your phone to keep yourself accountable.

Lesson 34: Social Selling

Before you cringe and ignore this marketing tip with the word 'selling' in the title, take a deep breath and remind yourself no one achieves anything without someone who initiates a sales process. Every day, you benefit by doing work for a client who someone, maybe even you, had to have a sales conversation.

Social selling is the strategic and consistent use of social media platforms to position yourself as an expert. If you have been ignoring social media, you are ignoring a massive platform from which to gain exactly the business you want. How would it feel to be able to turn away the crummy, difficult, and unprofitable projects because your pipeline is full of great clients and projects you love? Social selling has the potential to get you the clients and projects you want.

Here are a few tips for improving your social selling acumen.

• LinkedIn is the best social media channel for social selling design and construction services! If you are not using LinkedIn or rarely engage this dynamic and powerful tool, start using it regularly. (Refer to Lesson 19: Thought Leadership and LinkedIn).

- Social selling does not mean posting things about how great you are and how everyone who needs professional services should be hiring you. In fact, you rarely or never talk about yourself or your qualifications.

- Social selling means posting content from other experts. If you discover good content from other sources you know your clients and prospects will enjoy and learn from, share it.

- Social selling means reposting and sharing content from your clients and prospects to celebrate and applaud their successes and what they care about.

- The primary means of social selling is engagement. Simply engage your network of colleagues, business associates, clients, and prospects by liking, commenting, and sharing content.

- Regarding LinkedIn, only connect with people who either can hire your services, influence the buying decision, are experts in related or similar industries or are somehow connected to your industries. There is no need to clutter your network with people who have no connection, interest, or impact on your field of business.

For more detailed tips or training on developing your LinkedIn profile and executing an effective social selling strategy, ask for help. There are marketing consultants who specialize in social media who will get you going and assist you.

Challenge

For those of you not on LinkedIn or not using LinkedIn regularly, start *today!* Get your profile up and current. Use a professional head shot for your photo. *Yes,* you need a good photo on your profile. Set reminders or notifications at least once a week to check your news feed. Start engaging your network by liking and commenting on stories and posts of interest.

For those of you already utilizing LinkedIn, keep up the good work. Make sure your profile stays accurate. Do a deep dive and add your licenses, credentials, special recognitions, and awards. Follow companies with whom you do business or would like to do business. Research prospects and provide good content relative to your work.

Lesson 35: LinkedIn Company Pages

In August of 2020, my company (more accurately—'I') ramped up our marketing efforts utilizing LinkedIn. I started posting a variety of regular updates every week to engage our clients, prospects, and business associates. As of this writing, we are five months into actively engaging others on our company LinkedIn page. The results have been fantastic!

- We increased followers by 71% in five months from 338 to 472.

- Fifty-one (51) post updates in five months. Our engagement rate climbed from 5.93% in September to 9.58% in December. Engagement is measured by adding (clicks + likes + comments + shares + follows) divided by (total impressions).

  - Our company posts/updates realized 13,567 impressions. Of those impressions 7,139 were unique.

    o Impression = the number of times your posts/updates were shown to members.

    o Unique impression = the number of times your posts/updates were shown to individual members. This only counts a member once, even if they have seen the update multiple times.

  - Nine videos were posted ranging in content from project specific videos to general service highlights to an award presentation. The highest number of views for a single video was 285.

- Top three industries represented in our followers are Utilities (25.8%), Civil Engineering (11.4%), and Construction (8.11%).

- 41% of our followers are from our target client industries (Utilities, Architecture, Construction, Government Administration).

What these statistics represent is the awareness and engagement of LinkedIn members with my company. As I reviewed the members who follow my company, we have a variety of engineering students, construction professionals, engineers, utilities professionals, industry vendors, architects, municipal officials, economic developers, realtors, public works staff, banking, federal agencies, and professional associations. Staying top of mind and providing valuable, educational, and interesting content is social marketing 101!

My favorite takeaway from social media engagement on our company LinkedIn page came from two comments on a general services post regarding electrical substation projects. The comments were from an industry vendor and a construction manager. Both were applauding our work and one tagged a specific employee!

Challenge

If you have responsibility for your company's social media presence, utilize your LinkedIn company page. LinkedIn provides excellent analytics so you can gauge what works and what does not while engaging your network. For example, one lesson I have already learned is that posting several relevant photos with your content will increase engagement significantly.

If you do not have responsibility for your company's social media presence, or you have no social media presence, resolve to have this discussion with company leaders. Most leaders who are shy about a company social media presence are so because of perceived lack of control over the message. They worry about comments others will make or marketing staff making errors in messaging. It may slow down the process, but it is okay to agree to run your posts by certain leaders for approval before posting. I do this with any post that is project specific. I want to make sure I have my facts right and that we have permission to publicize a client's project.

Lesson 36: Seven Things Your Clients Want You to Know

The following is a summary of an article in *Marketer* (June 2020). You can retrieve the full article at www.smps.org.

There are some universal truths your clients want you to know. Specifically, here are seven areas on which you should focus in your client relationships. Each area has direct client quotes gleaned from Howard J. Wolff, FSMPS, the article's author.[21]

1 **Focus on helping, not selling!** "Listen harder. Communicate with a purpose. Let me know you have something worthy of my time and attention."

When you focus on helping, you may discover that the solution the client needs is not one you provide. Therefore, having a robust and diverse network is so important for great business developers. You are most helpful when you understand the client's need and know just the right person to offer a solution.

2 **Clients have a pretty good BS detector.** "Your reputation is as important as your portfolio … In doing our research, we first ask colleagues for recommendations; then we go to those firms' websites to look for relevant

experience. After seeing a project we like, we double check with that client to see how they felt about it."

You are not the only one doing your homework. Clients research your company and you! Clients want you to know they can smell your S#^T a mile away. Do not try and sell what you do not have. Do not try and be something you are not.

3 **Don't suck up. Speak up!** "My advice to designers, when they don't agree with where we're headed, is to say, 'We'll do what you want us to do, but we think you're on the wrong track and here's why' … Don't try to hide bad news and don't let it fester. Bad news doesn't improve with age. Tell us if something is wrong and get it out on the table early; otherwise, it will only get worse."

Unfortunately, I have witnessed engineers stick their heads in the sand when something goes wrong. I have also watched contractors and architects do the same. The best professionals understand the value in delivering bad news as soon as possible. They also know how to disagree with a client in a respectful and gentle manner. Clients want a partnership, not a dictatorship. Clients want leadership, not cowardice.

4. **Show me.** "Don't tell me you cannot do something. Find a way to do it. The art of problem-solving and design-thinking is getting lost."

This is a pet peeve of mine since I started marketing in the A/E/C industry seventeen years ago. I used to get so frustrated with engineer colleagues when I would bring a prospective client or project to them and their first words were how they could not do it. I believe it is equally irritating when clients hear how their project cannot be done.

My dad, who is a civil engineer, used to say, "Anything can be engineered, but it may cost too much to be realistic."

I often thought this to be a much better response to a perceived impossible project. Let the client know how it CAN be done first, then help them navigate the cost and let them decide how they wish to proceed.

5. **It's your job to know what I need.** "We want to see increasing detail on scope and spend alignment. Validate budget conformance from the start and through all phases of a project … Offer cost-containment alternatives that don't fundamentally alter the project."

I recognize marketers typically do not have much influence on a project scope and budget. However, this is good information to share with your project managers or those with responsibility over these contract items. Clients want to know what they are paying for and are becoming increasingly sophisticated in their knowledge of how projects are completed. Encourage your technical staff to educate their clients well on exactly what they are paying for.

6. **Your fee is not as important as you think it is.** "We don't always select the firm with the lowest fee, but it's hard to justify selecting someone whose fee is two or three times higher than the others … Don't play the game of low-balling a fee to get the job and then hitting us with additional services over and over."

Hiding fees or being vague about a final project cost is not good marketing. It is best practice to be up front about your fee and provide the best data supporting your fee. 'Buying' a project with low-ball fees to get a client on the hook and then charging additional fees is simply a dishonest tactic. This creates an adversarial relationship that causes everyone grief.

7. **Don't take us for granted.** "Recently, an incumbent firm seemed rather robotic in their presentation. In contrast, a short-listed firm with whom we had never worked had

their entire staff visit our facility and interview our staff. Then they shared their observations and recommendations. That was impressive. It said a lot about their interest and enthusiasm."

Every project is an opportunity to impress, even if the client has been with your firm for decades. Long-term loyal clients do not like being taken for granted. In this increasingly competitive environment, your client is also many other firms' prospect. And your competitors are becoming better at winning work. Account-based marketing is a valuable tool to keep sharp!

Challenge

Share these 'seven things clients want you to know' with your firm leaders. Follow up with them and ask questions about how they received it. Create opportunities for discussion around these topics and get your people thinking about what they need to do to keep clients satisfied.

Lesson 37: The Loyalty Ladder

As marketers and business developers, one of the greatest challenges we face is measuring success. When it comes to client relationships and the strategies it takes to win new work, an effective measurement tool is the Loyalty Ladder. It's a five-step process focused on moving a client through the various relationship levels, starting with qualified leads who have an opportunity to hire firms for services all the way to loyal brand champions who will advocate for a firm in their sphere of influence.

In the late 1990s, marketing theorist Adrian Payne developed the Relationship Ladder as a concept that clients can be transformed from cold potential buyers into loyal supporters of a brand. The five stages he identified are Prospect, Customer, Client, Supporter, and Advocate.

In the A/E/C industries, these same principles apply and are an excellent foundation for mapping your client journey while engaging all players at our firms—from marketing to business developers to technical staff—to actively participate in bringing business to our firms. We do this through transitioning our relationships from prospects to advocates:

Prospects: Prospects have a need for your firm's services, and with that comes the potential opportunity to hire your firm. While the prospect may have familiarity with your firm, typically there's no existing relationship. Prospects are identified as part of BD strategy, based on client personas, with a corresponding client-capture plan for each potential client.

Awareness: Once a prospect is identified, marketing and BD kick into high gear and work collaboratively to raise brand awareness. Brand awareness is the level to which your brand is recognized by potential clients and associated with your firm's service and/or people. Seth Godin said he believes building a valuable brand includes building, "the most predictable, emotional experience you can among those that care about you." The focus of marketing is to ensure consistent brand experience to engage the prospect into becoming a client.

Trust: Trust begins when a client invites a firm to engage or when a firm is hired. Through focused brand awareness campaigns, the client becomes aware what's special about your services, experience, and expertise and believes you can provide the best solutions for their company or project.

Loyalty: Loyalty is all about repeat business. According to the White House Office of Consumer Affairs, it costs six to seven times more to acquire new clients than to retain current ones. *Harvard Business Review* reports that increasing customer retention by 5% can increase profits 25% to 95%.

Advocacy: When you reach advocacy, your clients rave about your services and encourage others to trust you. They have enough trust in your firm to promote your firm to prospects, provide testimonials, and generally help you expand your client base.

Moving a client from prospect to advocate takes work. The most successful client relationships take persistence, time, and effort to be effective. Following a process like the Loyalty Ladder helps ensure you are intentional and allows your firm to measure its success.[22]

(Article by SMPS Past President Doug Parker, FSMPS, CPSM, principal of Elevate Marketing Advisors. He can be reached at doug@elevatemarketingadvisors.com)

Use the following Loyalty Ladder to identify at least one client at each level of the ladder. Once you have identified a client for each level, follow the challenge advice at each level to move your client up the ladder.

Prospects: May or may not be aware of your firm, but they regularly hire services your firm provides.

Challenge: Reach out to them in the next seven days asking about their organization, role, and needs. Do not sell; just learn more about them. If they respond, be sure to thank them.

Awareness: Prospect is aware of your firm and has had minimal interaction, but has never hired your firm's services.

Challenge: In the next seven days, send marketing collateral that is applicable to their organization and needs and request a brief visit or lunch to discuss their organizational goals.

Trust: The client has hired your firm for the first time in the last twelve months.

Challenge: In the next seven days, request a debrief visit or lunch. Ask the client some simple questions about their experience working with your firm and what you can do better.

Loyalty: The client orders repeated work and has a high level of trust in your services. They may hire your firm for several types of work.

Challenge: In the next seven days, send a hand-written thank-you note and appropriate gift card thanking them for their loyalty and continued business. Ask them in the note if they know of a similar organization that could benefit from our services and if they are willing to make a referral.

Advocacy: The client is a long-time repeat client who uses your firm exclusively or almost exclusively. The client also refers your services to others.

Challenge: Call the client and thank them for their loyalty and advocacy of your services. Tell them you would like to show your appreciation with a nice dinner at a place of their choosing or set up a time to grill burgers and hot dogs for their office staff.

Lesson 38: The Journey to a Solution

Strategy is more important than solutions. To our clients, the solution to their infrastructure problems is not as important as the journey they take with you to that solution. Assuming that the infrastructure solution is fairly equal among all competitors, then the journey to that solution is what matters to the client. Every project is a journey and the professional who makes the client's journey the easiest and most rewarding will win more work and more loyalty.

So what differentiates one professional from another? The solutions are relatively the same. Differentiators are the characteristics of the journey. These include speed, ease, cooperative problem solving, creative funding, communication, responsiveness, regulatory compliance, innovative delivery, contractor cooperation, and budget. On these attributes of the journey, the client's experience from one professional to another can be dramatically different.

While every good professional should be focused on the technical solution, remember you are hired based on the perceived journey of your client. What could you be doing differently to make their journey easier and more rewarding?

Challenge

In the second paragraph of this lesson, I listed ten attributes of a client's journey through a design project. These attributes need to be measured and emphasized to stand out from your competition. Let us consider each of them individually and a possible challenge with each attribute.

1. **Speed**. What can you tweak or change to create better efficiency in your project deliverables?

2. **Ease**. Imagine you are the client. At every point of interaction with your firm, what could you do to make that interaction easier?

3. **Cooperative problem-solving**. Do you engage your client to brainstorm possible solutions with you? Can you do something that would better engage clients to solve their own problems?

4. **Creative funding**. Do you educate yourself and your staff on potential funding sources for your projects? Have you considered coordinating several stakeholders to help you get projects funded?

5. **Communication**. In what ways do you regularly stay in communication with your clients, especially when there is no active project? Are you committed to responding to client requests within 24 hours or less?

6. **Responsiveness**. Related to #5, how easy is it for clients to contact you? Do you return calls promptly? Do you read and respond to emails promptly?

7. **Regulatory compliance**. Do you and your staff stay educated and current on all regulatory issues related to your projects? Are you nurturing your business relationships with regulatory agencies?

8. **Innovative delivery**. Do you and your staff stay educated on project delivery methods? Do you ever take time to consider alternate delivery methods that would benefit the client?

9. **Contractor cooperation**. As an architect or engineer, do you nurture your business relationships with contractors who regularly bid your projects? Do you communicate as effectively with contractors as you do your clients?

10. **Budget**. Do you work internally to streamline processes, keep software updated, advance your technology to create better efficiencies? Do you manage project budgets with the same attention to detail as your design deliverables?

Lesson 39: Reactive vs. Proactive

When it comes to business development and selling professional services, there are two primary strategies most firms employ: Reactive and Proactive. I would like to make the case that one strategy is clearly better than the other.

Reactive business development is mostly about the preparation of marketing collateral to respond to business opportunities. This strategy looks at the market as a conglomeration of clients and prospects who will have projects and issue an RFQ/RFP when they are ready for services. Being reactive means waiting for the RFQ/RFP and preparing the best qualifications we can for responding to the RFQ/RFP.

Proactive business development is about staying 'top of mind' and positioning your people and firm as the best option for clients and prospects. Before the client issues an RFQ/RFP, proactive firms are already aware of the project and are already working to position themselves to win trust and confidence. This is accomplished by strategic and consistent 'marketing touches' with the client.

I believe proactive business development is a better strategy. While reactive selling works, it does not work as well. When employing proactive strategies hit rates go up and firms typically win work with preferred clients and on preferred projects.

Here are some proactive strategies for you to consider:

1. Storytelling. When interacting with clients or prospects, always be prepared with several strong stories of how you helped similar clients solve similar problems. Learn how to tell a good story without sounding self-promoting or salesy. (Refer to Lesson 11: Storytelling)

2. Interact Online: Use your social media platforms, especially LinkedIn, to connect with clients and prospects. Interact with them and provide valuable content. Like and share company news and posts. (Refer to Lesson 34: Social Selling.)

3. Solve Problems for Free: When it makes sense and is relatively easy, solve a problem for the client/prospect for free. If the client has a small engineering-related issue you can solve with little effort or time, do it and do not charge.

4. Cross-Sell: Learn how to listen for 'other' problems or issues the client/prospect has. It is easy to stay focused on what you are doing for the client and disregard issues that are out of your realm of skill. Pay attention and introduce other experts who can solve a problem you cannot, especially if that expert is another of your firm's employees! (Refer to Lesson 4: Cross-Marketing)

5. Cold Call Established Clients: *Noooo*! I used the phrase 'cold call' and probably lost most of you. Hear me out. When you call on an established client, it really isn't cold-calling; it's warm calling. You know your clients well enough to know which ones would appreciate a surprise phone call or drop in and which would not. For those who will accept it, pop in on them occasionally with some morning doughnuts or bag of bagels and say hello.

Challenge

This is an easy one. Pick one of the five proactive business development strategies and do it within the next seven days.

Chapter 4 – Project Management

Lesson 40: Project Data

Project data is a marketer's arsenal for better marketing, customer engagement, and business development. What do I mean by project data? Project data includes the components of a project or its size. These include how many linear feet of gravity sewer line were installed, how many tons of asphalt were laid, or how many miles of 110kv line were designed. This project data is static and tells a portion of the project story. The static project data gives the client a sense of the size and maybe complexity of a given project. But what most engineering firms miss in marketing is the dynamic data.

Dynamic project data goes beyond the components that describe size or complexity. Project data such as the difference between an engineer's estimate of construction cost, the construction bid, and the final construction cost tells a dynamic story about cost estimating accuracy, budget alignment, and design plan accuracy. Or, for example, how aware was the owner of project design milestones? Was the owner able to know exactly where the design team was on construction plan development and if this was ahead, on, or behind schedule? What was the story of owner communication?

The ability to showcase results as they happen, rather than after they happen, can differentiate a project team in real time.

So how do we capture, understand, communicate, and highlight dynamic project data? Here's an example:

One of my firm's principals forwarded an email to me from a utility director at a client company. We were performing a design for water system expansion. Part of our responsibility was to obtain approval from Missouri State Historical Preservation Office regarding an easement across Missouri Department of Conservation property. We produced approval quickly and received this response from the utility director:

"Wow! You guys are efficient plus 10."

I attached this email and quote to our Client Relationship Management (CRM) system record for that client and specific contact for future reference. Now we have a brief story to tell that demonstrates our efficiency in permitting, working with multiple Missouri agencies, and keeping projects on schedule.

The key to capturing, understanding, communicating, and highlighting dynamic project data is to share your data with marketing. Meaningful correspondence with clients, project innovations that save time and/or money, process efficiencies, use of technology that saves time and/or money, etc., are all good dynamic project data! All you must do is share it.

Challenge

The challenge for design professionals is to recognize dynamic project data and share it with your marketing staff. Do you have closeout documents or a standard process for closing a project? If so, simply look for dynamic project data during closeout and add those items as part of the process.

The challenge for marketers is to help your technical staff, recognize dynamic project data, and make it easy for them to report that data. I send out a one-page Project Completion Form at the end of every month to all project managers. This form has space to add both static and dynamic project data. (See Appendix B)

Whether you are a design professional or marketer, take a moment to audit your closeout documents or create an easy way to report dynamic project data.

Lesson 41: Project Follow-Ups

One best practice for gaining referrals and finding the next project with a successful client is post-project follow-up. While the thought of asking for more work right on the heels of a successful project closeout may seem pushy or inappropriate, doing it well will not be pushy at all. In fact, if done correctly, your client will enjoy talking with you and appreciate the initiative to learn more about them, their organization, and where you fit in to help.

A sample email to send post-project can be found in Appendix C. This would only be used following a successful project in which you know the client is happy. Notice the sections of the email and the intent. You are not requesting more work. You are not trying to sell them anything. You are demonstrating appreciation, value, hope, and enjoyment. Rephrase the example email to sound like you and follow the outline. Once you gain an appointment with your client, use the following questions to guide your conversation:

• Can you tell me more about (what worked so well)? Try to use their words about the project. For example, can you tell me more about finishing ahead of schedule and why that was important to you?

- What about your situation made this outcome good?

- Who else in your organization was affected by this project?

- How else can we help you and your organization?

- Can you tell me more about that (referring to question 4)?

- What would an ideal engineer do that no one does now?

- Are there others, like you, who need this kind of help? If yes, would you be willing to make an introduction to discover if we may be helpful to them as well?

Utilizing this post-project approach will help you find more work. This work may come from the satisfied client or by referral. Either way, you are building your reputation as a successful helper who listens, understands, and solves clients' problems.

Challenge

Pick a successful recent project you completed. Utilize the example email in Appendix C and write an email to that client requesting a follow-up. Do in the next seven days.

Lesson 42: Project Pursuits

There are three key steps to creating a successful project pursuit strategy.

1. Before the RFQ/RFP shows up, know the client. Too many teams focus all their energy on the project's obvious needs like budget and schedule. But what is the 'big picture' of the project? Why is the client doing this particular project at this particular time? What is truly driving this project to be completed? Keep asking the "so that ... "questions. For example, the client wants to make improvements to their wastewater treatment plant to improve capacity and effluent quality … "so that" … the city can continue to grow and attract additional industrial development and attract labor and economic development. Know the end goal of why the project is being pursued!

2. Know the competition. Don't obsess about the competition, but certainly don't ignore this information either. Simply discover with whom you will most likely be competing and do a simple S.W.O.T. analysis. **S**trengths. **W**eaknesses. **O**pportunities. **T**hreats. Perform the S.W.O.T analysis on your own firm as well as the competing firms. Once completed, highlight and emphasize your strengths, in particular your strengths as compared to your competitors, and compensate for your weaknesses. Do not spend more than 30-40 minutes on this step.

3. Develop a unique strategy. In order to develop a unique strategy you must honestly think about and answer the following questions:

a. What can we say and do that our competitors cannot?

b. What specific lesson learned from past projects will be applied to this project?

c. How will our work on this project contribute to solving the client's biggest needs or concerns?

The selection committee typically already knows 'what' you do. Your strategy is not unique if it is to regurgitate your years in business and how excited you are to work on their project. Your strategy is unique when you explain how you will perform using real steps, people, places, and processes. Do not just say you will be on time and within budget. Demonstrate how you will schedule the project and spend their money efficiently.

Going through these steps will help you nail down an effective strategy for pursuing your next project. Do not sound like all your competitors. Be different and approach your next project with a special focus to executing a specific strategy that is directly related to the end goals of the client's project.

Challenge

Some projects are too small or inconsequential to go through a complete project pursuit strategy. However, there are plenty of larger projects where this strategy will be of benefit. Do not let yourself get in the boilerplate rut saying the same thing all the time. If you execute these three pursuit strategy steps, you will discover how to tailor message your proposal.

To practice, take a former proposal or qualifications statement that has already been completed and rework it applying these three steps. Apply your "so that … " questions. Perform the S.W.O.T competitive analysis. Create your unique messaging. I believe you will discover improvements and things you wish you would have said differently. This practice will help you on the next RFQ/RFP when it really counts!

Lesson 43: Responsiveness! The Secret Sauce

When my father instituted a policy for project managers (PM) to help them be more responsive to clients, he asked every PM to write a monthly letter to every active client. The letter was to explain where they were in the project schedule, how much budget had been spent, how much was left (if applicable), and what the client could expect from them in the next month. It was a simple status report.

Several months into this new policy, one project manager replied during our monthly PM meeting that he had not written to two of his clients because nothing had been done on their project for that month. There was nothing to report. In a very calm but direct manner, my dad paused the meeting and explained why we were writing the letters. Even if nothing was completed for the month, it was vitally important that the client know there was nothing completed, and more importantly—why.

I tell this story because it points out a secret marketing power you have as a project manager. The power is responsive communication with your clients. Keeping your clients well-informed does several things.

1. Well-informed clients have peace of mind that you are thinking about their project, and therefore, feel important as a client.

2. Well-informed clients are not left to their own imaginations as to why certain tasks take longer than others or why one month's invoice is much larger than another month. They know exactly why, which helps them feel more in control of their own project.

3. Well-informed clients learn something about their projects and how they get engineered and built. This makes your client feel smart and part of the process.

If you'd like your clients to feel important, in control, and smart, then keep them informed and stay ahead of the responsiveness curve. How smart do you look when you answer their questions before they even ask them?

Challenge

The easy challenge would be to ask that you set a recurring date on your calendar to send all your active clients a status report once a month. This could be as easy as a quick email that simply highlights schedule, budget, and plan for next month. You can do that and be effective. However, if you want to make a significant impression, send a physical letter or hand-written note.

Lesson 44: Three Competitive Pricing Tactics

Are you being outbid by competitors on price proposals? You may assume too many firms are simply 'buying' projects. But procurement by our clients is a game. Maybe you just aren't very good at the game yet?

Here are three competitive pricing tactics to consider to up your procurement game.

1. **Play a different game.** If a client's procurement practices force you to work at a loss, why are you working with that client? There may be a good reason. However, sometimes the reason is, *This is a long-standing client who always gives us work.* Rethink this strategy because clients like this often slowly bleed our business and steal our joy in our work. Find clients who can pay your fees. If you have big league fees stop playing in the minor leagues.

2. **Staff the project differently.** It is unwise to leave pricing to the end. Think about the price and staff the project accordingly. You must walk the line between showing the right qualifications and providing a price that is competitive. Why offer a client a $75,000 solution when a $55,000 solution will work just fine?

3. **Bid the (real) scope.** The scope identified in an RFP does not always align with the client's real needs or wants. Understanding the difference between the published scope and the real scope enables you to respond with a written scope price and an alternative price that reflects the real scope. This also shows your superior knowledge of the client and their budget. Just be careful that the two proposed bids are correctly identified with the different scopes so you are not stuck designing the published scope with the alternative price.

Engineers do not like bidding for projects. However, there are reasons why it must be done. When pricing a job strategically, competitively priced projects can still be enjoyable and profitable.

Challenge

Do some reading and studying on buying psychology. Blair Enns, Author and CEO, *Win Without Pitching*[23], has some good material regarding buying psychology and value pricing consultative services. Additionally, the SMPS Foundation published a whitepaper by Jonrobert Tartaglione titled, "The Neuropsychology of Influence and Decision-Making."[24] In it, Mr. Tartaglione presents the psychology of contrast effects. He explains how offering contrasting prices and levels of quality have a 'middling' effect. Buyers will gravitate toward a middle option.

Take the time to do your own research and discover how you can not only value price your services but present your price options for the optimal result.

Lesson 45: Managing Expectations

Our industry is not known for our detailed and eloquent messaging skills, and that is perfectly okay. We are trained to be scientists and engineers first, and communications often takes a back seat. But when it comes to making sure our clients are ultimately happy with what we do—which, let's admit it, is the point of this whole thing—we must be effective educators and communicators despite our innate discomfort or unwillingness. Firmly incorporated within our responsibilities for technical projects is the obligation to accurately communicate what we do and why we are doing it, to build consensus and understanding, and most importantly, to make sure that the client is aligned with our objectives throughout the process. That way, when we achieve successes, both big and small, the client will appreciate them and be pleased with the outcome.

Of course, this critical part of all projects usually is not written into the technical specifications or the construction sequence. We need to make a special effort to manage expectations by incorporating these strategies into our project execution:

- **Be realistic from the start.** Sure, we all want to tell our clients about our great work. But it's one thing for you to say, "We'll design an excellent building," and far, far another to promise, "The builder will construct this in half the time." A shortened construction timeline may be what you both are hoping for, but the wise professional knows what variables may lie ahead and doesn't get caught up in expectational exuberance.

- **Keep a level head.** Have you ever started to see good results in the early stages of a project, only to see conflicting or negative results in its later stages? We've all been there; we get caught up in the early good news and can't wait to start our cheerleading routine in front of the client. Our optimism is infectious, and is hugely important, but until we know all the data, we can't know 100 percent of the outcome. So instead, we must temper mid-project good news and act with restraint. And while that may be less exciting to deliver or for the client to hear, it's much more responsible professional behavior.

- **Check in early and often.** One of the biggest mistakes we as professionals can make is to get too far along a project timeline without checking in with the client. Remember, our clients are often in a dynamic environment and their needs and goals could evolve over the course of a project. We need to re-calibrate with them often to make sure that we're moving in parallel. If we fail to do this, we risk leaving an understanding gap that could lead to disappointment at the end of the project. (David Coyne, The Zweig Letter, January 27, 2020)[25]

Challenge

This is simply a good reminder from David Coyne to level our expectations. I find this is most helpful to the marketers who tend to over-exaggerate or over-promise. A good challenge is for both technical staff and marketers to talk with each other consistently enough to make sure all the messaging coming from your firm is consistent.

Lesson 46: Project Updates with Clients

Updating or checking in with our clients during project execution is often overlooked. It is a critical element to a successful project. Here are a few tips on how to implement an effective and strategic client update or check-in plan.

- Identify who the actual 'buyer' is for the project. It's important to know exactly who is paying the bills and making the decisions regarding your project. Your day-to-day interactions may be with internal staff of the client's organization who are not decision-makers. Know who the primary decision-maker or buyer is and plan to update that person.

- At the initial scoping meeting for the project, decide on a cadence for updating the buyer. A good rule of thumb is to divide the project schedule into fifths. Whatever the expected schedule, plan on specific dates and times for project updates that is agreeable to both you and your buyer. If the buyer wishes for more frequent updates, negotiate those updates and adjust your budget accordingly. A more appropriate update cadence may correspond with project milestones. They don't have to fit neatly into fifths.

- Formal cadence for project updates doesn't mean you can't talk with the buyer for other purposes. You will likely have more interaction with the buyer than your planned update meetings. Leave space for this and expect dialogue between the formal meetings.

- Include three key discussion points in your update meetings. Progress, challenges, and next steps. Update the progress you've made thus far. Describe any challenges you are experiencing with the project and what you are doing about them. Go over your next steps until your next progress meeting.

If you do not plan and set aside time for project updates, it is too easy to 'go dark' during a project. Clients wish to be updated and understand where you are in your progress. Even challenges to the budget or schedule must be communicated as soon as possible. These updates will serve to keep both you and your client fueled toward success.

Effective and strategic project updates improve the client experience. This makes it more likely for you to be hired for future work and grow your client's trust in you as their expert!

Challenge

Look at a few of your projects and key client accounts. Make sure you know the answers to the following questions: Who holds the purse strings in the client organization? How often do your clients want you to update them? When was the last time you had a visit with your client, during an active project, that had nothing to do with the project? When you do give an update, do you cover progress, challenges, and next steps?

Lesson 47: Value Pricing vs. Billable Hour

Price the Client, Not the Job

Charging an hourly rate pushes the risk onto the client. What if you set a price based on the value or outcome? Now you as the consultant assume more risk. When you assume more risk, you are acting more like a business partner and less like a vendor. A price for an engineering task should be based on the value of that service to the client.

Efficiency Comes at the Cost of Increased Profits

Innovation and efficiency are opposed to each other. You increase one at the expense of the other. True value comes through innovation, which is a time-consuming and messy process. In pursuit of efficiency, you sacrifice time to think creatively, the freedom to fail.

Pricing Creativity

Offer options and anchor high. This means when proposing business to a client, offer several pricing and delivery options and anchor the first option extremely high. Follow the first option with two or three lower-priced options. Everyone has an 'extremist aversion,' which means they will gravitate toward an option in the middle. The highest anchor price is not there to sell but to make a comparison, so a middle option is chosen. The lowest option should be the billable hour. All other options should be based on value.

Master the Value Conversation

What does the client want? What will we measure? What is this worth to the client? What would the client pay for this? These questions drive what the conversation should look like when pricing a client. Notice the conversation is centered on them, their project, their needs, their desired outcome.

Disclaimer: I understand not all engineering projects fit into a value-pricing model. However, more jobs do than you think! What projects/clients can you think of that are more conducive to value pricing?

This content was adapted from the book *Pricing Creativity: A Guide to Profit Beyond the Billable Hour*, by Blair Enns.[26]

Challenge

Audit your clients and pick out the ones you believe are good candidates for value pricing. Not all markets are created equal, so some consultants may find this challenge difficult, if not impossible. But I contend there are more clients who would be better served and receptive to value pricing than we might think.

Lesson 48: Selling Time or Value?

Which is better, selling time or value? Seriously! Think about that question for a moment.

If you sell your time, what are the advantages and disadvantages? If you sell value, what are the advantages and disadvantages?

In nearly all our projects, we typically sell our time. We structure many of our contracts according to how much of our time we are selling. We have an hourly rate schedule that identifies what we propose to bill per hour of an employee's time. We estimate engineering fees based on how much time we think it will require for our teams to fulfill the client's needs. When we sell our time we are selling a limited resource. When we sell a limited resource we limit revenue and profit potential.

What if we learned how to sell our value? Here's a scenario to illustrate:

As an engineer, you provide consultation for a project and it took you 15 hours of your time. You charge $194/hour and bill the project $2,910 ($194 x 15 = $2,910). The client thanks you for the work, pays your bill, and says you did a good job. The client asks you to do the same type of work for three more similar projects, only this time it takes you 11 hours per project. Billing time would earn you $6,402 ($194 x 11 = $2,134; 3 projects x $2,134 = $6,402). At the project price of $2,910 done in 11 hours, you increase your billing value and earn $8,730 ($2,910 x 3 projects = $8,370). The client 'valued' your first project at $2,910. Why would you charge less than what the client values?

Many tasks we do are repetitive that yield efficiency. When you learn to design efficiently, you can either give that efficiency value to the client or profit from that efficiency allowing you more time for other projects.

Some clients request itemized billing invoices that reflect your time. In such cases, you are either stuck billing only for your time or you can renegotiate your contract and invoicing requirements. What repetitive and efficient tasks can you itemize as a task completed rather than hours billed? When can you utilize a lump sum contract to maximize your efficiencies?

Challenge

Perform an audit of your projects over the past six months. Which of these projects could you have billed for value rather than time? Which projects are repetitive that yield better efficiencies? Do you have opportunities with specific clients to renegotiate from an hourly billing to a task completed contract? I hope you will discover opportunities to sell your value and not only your time. You will find the work more rewarding while keeping your client satisfied.

Lesson 49: Turning Down Work is Good Marketing

I've been reminded a few times lately that it is sometimes a good marketing decision to turn down work. Saying no to certain clients and projects is a good marketing strategy for several reasons.

1. Working for clients who only want low bid work see engineering or architecture as just another commodity, or worse, a necessary evil to get through a project. Do you want to be a commodity or a necessary evil?

2. Some clients love scope creep! They love to get you contracted for one scope of work, only to change and add scope tasks but expect not to be billed for the extra work. Do you want to keep working on projects that lose money?

3. The client and project may be a great fit, but you know from the beginning you cannot make their timeline or stay within their budget. You either tell them this upfront and let them decide on still hiring you, or you gently pass and let them know that while you would enjoy working for them, you just cannot take on their project at this time.

4. You have a great client who asks you to do a project you know is outside your level of expertise. You know enough to 'get by,' but also recognize there are other consultants who would do a much better job. Help the client find the right consultant to do the job.

Good marketing does not allow engineering and architecture services to be commoditized or viewed as a necessary evil. Good marketing means completing profitable projects and getting paid for your expertise. Good marketing is being honest and open about what you can and cannot do. Good marketing is staying within your ability and not trying to be all things to all clients.

Challenge

These are just a few good reasons to turn down work. There are many more depending on your specific design or construction niche. Come up with three to five more questions that will help you determine when it may be a good idea to turn down work.

Chapter 5 – Professional Development

Lesson 50: Virtual Meetings

Of course, you had to know this was coming. Because we are communicating more often via virtual platforms, it is worthwhile to review good virtual meeting etiquette and best practices.

1. Log in to the meeting platform a few minutes early. Be a good manager of your time. There's nothing wrong with logging in early and then continuing to work on something else while you wait for the meeting to start. Like a face-to-face meeting, no one likes repeating themselves because someone showed up late.

2. Mute your microphone. If you are not the meeting organizer, mute your microphone immediately. Keep your mic muted until you need to speak. Once you are finished speaking mute your mic again. This requires discipline and focus. The side benefit is it keeps you focused on the meeting and not other tasks.

3. Let the meeting organizer control the conversation. Remember the manners your parents taught you when you were a kid? Do not speak unless you are spoken to. This was our parents' teaching us how to behave in a social situation with others who are in authority over us. The meeting organizer is the authority, so do not speak unless the

organizer speaks to you. This also applies if you need to speak to a participant other than the organizer. Let the organizer facilitate who is supposed to be speaking to whom.

4. Try to conduct your meeting in a private space with minimal distraction. Do you best to join a virtual meeting in a space with minimal or no other noises. Background noise, especially when you forget to mute yourself, will ruin the communication for everyone. Also remember to minimize or eliminate visual distractions such as pets, children, television, etc.

Following these best practices demonstrates that you are thinking of others before yourself. Ignoring them demonstrates that you are either lazy, incompetent, or intentionally obnoxious! Practice these protocols to love your neighbor as yourself.

Challenge

On your next virtual call put a sticky note with these four reminders on your screen. Abbreviate these best practices so you can easily and quickly remember what behaviors are encouraged. Honestly, if you are thinking more of the other virtual participants than you are thinking about how your hair looks, you will do fine. Put others before yourself and you will be a good virtual guest.

Lesson 51: Tools for Success

There are several options when it comes to organization tools to help you succeed. When you are in the consulting business you work with numerous clients and projects simultaneously. Therefore, it is essential that you manage your time and resources wisely. Here are a few tools for you to consider in keeping organized.

- **Use Outlook to its maximum potential.** Most Outlook users are barely scratching the surface of this tool's full capabilities. For email correspondence, Outlook allows you to create folders, set reminders for responding, track open and read receipts, color categorize, file in OneNote, or convert to a PDF. For calendar and appointments Outlook allows you to view other network users' schedules, add meeting notes from OneNote, use Scheduling Assistant to plan a meeting, set a recurring meeting, color categorize, invite attendees. I use an add-on called Grammarly which reviews my emails for spelling and best grammar practices. There are multiple add-ons available that may assist your organization and keep you on track.

- **LinkedIn.com.** This may be a surprise, but LinkedIn.com is a goldmine for many business activities. You can research prospects and clients (by person or company). Educate yourself with articles or follow professional associations. Use hashtags to research specific topics and trends. On the Premium paid side of LinkedIn, you can take advantage of thousands of learning modules specific to business. You can learn from topics such as presentations, project management, strategic thinking, time management, networking, etc. I use LinkedIn to keep expanding my professional network, research prospects and clients, keep up with industry trends and best practices, and learn how to do my job better!

- **CRM for marketing leads and opportunity tracking.** Whether you utilize a CRM tool or not, you may want to know the possible uses of CRM. You can track project leads and opportunities. This builds a database of business intelligence that helps you make better decisions on which projects provide the best opportunities for rewarding work and profit. You may also track which proposals are won and lost, building a history so you can see how marketing efforts are either successful or need revised.

Challenge

These three tools—Outlook, LinkedIn, and CRM—are basic to most A/E/C businesses. Take full advantage of what is available to help you stay organized and efficient. I challenge you to research at least one of these tools to discover what features you are not currently using and learn how to utilize it.

Lesson 52: Presentations: Speak from Your Heart

When you're putting together your content for a presentation, do you ever say to yourself:

- What am I supposed to say?
- What do they want me to say?
- I need to sound professional.
- I must sound smooth and polished.

I call these our 'oughts' and 'shoulds.' Why do these thoughts fly through our heads? We are all looking for approval from our leaders, peers, and clients. This concern is so normal. What's tragic, however, is we often don't even realize we're stuck in these restrictive thought patterns. These *oughts* and *shoulds* are insidious, and can steal our voice and lock us up.

Let's look at it from the audience's perspective.

Who are those speakers you find impossible to resist? Who are the ones you could listen to all day long? Aren't they the ones who speak their truth with abandon and speak from a place of authenticity with a pure voice? They're real, they're raw, and maybe even a little messy. Their sincerity, their rawness, their humanness captures you. You somehow connect with them personally on a very human level. So, how can we get to that place of truth, abandon, and authenticity?

How can we put an end to the oughts and shoulds? Start here: When you're home alone and soul-searching for your content, ask yourself:

"How do I *feel* about my topic?" (Be honest.)

"Off the record, what would I *really* like to say to these people?"

Nine times out of ten, **your truth is exactly what will meet the needs of your listeners**, but we don't trust speaking that openly. "NO! It's not professional enough." "It's not interesting enough." "It's just not good enough." Lies. Lies. Lies. So, *now* what to do? Bring *all* your good, real, raw ideas and passion to your team rehearsal and let them hear it.

Trust your team. What will happen will amaze you! Your colleagues will applaud you, and they will have the right perspective to let you know if you've gone too far. Truth is, other people can edit our content or 'clean us up.' We can't clean ourselves up; we don't have the right perspective, and we get all up in our heads. The result? A stiff, boring presentation. So, trust your teammates.

Bottom line: **great presenting is a balance between speaking truth from your heart with a steadfast commitment to serving your audience's needs**. Speak your truth, help your listeners, and trust your team. Your *oughts* and *shoulds* won't stand a chance. (Carol Doscher, President & CEO at Graceworksinc.com)[27]

Challenge

This may be one of the hardest challenges yet. I want you to video record yourself giving a mock presentation. Set up a camera or your smartphone and speak as though the room were full of people. It will be awkward. You will stumble and stammer. That's okay; do it anyway. Then comes the harder part. Watch the video! This is the single best exercise I have undertaken to improve my presentation skills. You will notice all your bad habits and it will be excruciating. Do it anyway because the pain will motivate improvement.

Lesson 53: Busy vs. Productive

It may not be a direct correlation to marketing, but here are a few tips on how to be productive and not just busy. If you find yourself feeling behind, unable to keep up, or making frequent mistakes in your work, learn to be more productive and less busy.

• Cut your to-do list thoughtfully in half. You most likely have more on your to-do list than you can do in a day's work. Prioritize what is most important and cut the rest or move them to a different day.

• Categorize your assignments into 'urgent' and 'important.' Spend most of your time on what is urgent and save the 'important' stuff for later or tomorrow or next week.

• Create systems that block out distractions and keep you focused. For example, close your email unless you are focused on email. Turn off phone notifications.

• Know when to shut the door or put up a sign that requests others not to interrupt. On complex tasks that require high focus and energy, allow yourself to get into the zone and put a good 45 minutes in before allowing your concentration to be broken.

• Take necessary breaks. Your brain and body need to be refreshed throughout the day. Get away from your desk and walk, listen to some music, chat with a colleague, grab a snack.

For a more thorough reading, check out *The Differences Between Busy and Productive People*, by Larry Kim.[28]

Challenge

What is the biggest distraction in your office or workspace that prevents you from getting into the 'zone?' Whatever that distraction, plan to eliminate it. Your plan may mean turning off your phone notifications (including the vibrations and blinking lights). You may have to put a blunt sign on your cubicle that clearly says, DO NOT DISTURB! You may need to invest in some noise-cancelling headphones. Whatever you need to do, do it!

Lesson 54: What is the Difference Between Marketing and Business Development

The terms 'marketing' and 'business development' often get interchanged and very few know the difference. These are two interrelated functions that feed off each other but are not the same thing.

Marketing is:

1. The process of creating firm awareness,

2. Building and differentiating the brand,

3. Driving business development activities,

4. Identifying, anticipating, and satisfying client objectives to achieve profitable business goals.

Business development is a component of marketing, the process of identifying clients and opportunities, developing relationships, and securing profitable work for the firm.

Why is this important? Because marketing is the driving force that creates strategy and executes a mission to help make a company productive and profitable. Marketing is a business-centric activity. As such, the marketing team is typically a specific and identifiable group of people whose sole job function is directly tied to marketing tasks.

Business development is a function under the umbrella of marketing. While there may or may not be dedicated employees to the business development function, everyone who has any client-facing responsibility participates in business development. There are dedicated employees to business development, which occupies nearly all their time and energy. These full-time business development professionals' primary function is to create opportunities and open doors for business. The business development role of nurturing client relationships and closing deals falls to the project managers and leaders of the firm. While business development and marketing professionals assist in nurturing or closing deals, these are best accomplished by those who are performing the engineering tasks and managing projects.

You play a pivotal role in the success of driving business for our company. All your client interactions are marketing and business development. Every phone conversation, email and meeting are contributing to your firm's brand, driving future business opportunities, fulfilling or discovering client expectations, nurturing relationships and so on.

Challenge

If you are a design professional, take some time to get to know your marketing and business development staff. Ask them questions and find out more about their day-to-day jobs. If you are a full-time marketer or business developer, learn how to better incorporate technical staff in your activities. Find creative ways to get them engaged with your tasks.

Lesson 55: Are Your Conclusions Correct?

What? How? Why?

These are the three questions you need to be asking before drawing your conclusions.

When communicating with your clients, contractors, sub-consultants, vendors, and colleagues, it is human nature to make incorrect conclusions. When we assume what others mean we set the stage for miscommunication and problems.

1   Always ask people to define their terms. (What?)

"Human language is messy. The more a word is used, the more nuances of meaning it takes on. We will speak with people who use very familiar words, but with very different functional definitions." (Paul Tripp, "Getting To Know People," *Instruments In The Redeemer's Hands*)[9]

For example, you are speaking with a vendor who says, "The contractor is impossible." How you define impossible is likely different than how the vendor defines impossible. This is when you need to ask *What*. "What do you mean when you say the contractor is impossible?" What is impossible to you may look like a contractor who is stubborn, unyielding, and unresponsive. But when you ask the vendor what impossible means, they say impossible means the contractor had to reject some of their materials and it was going to cost the vendor money to correct it.

2   Always ask people to clarify what they mean with concrete, real life examples. (How?)

"If point (1) asked for their personal dictionary definition, then point (2) asks people to play us the video. The terms people use are verbal shorthand for significant situations." (Tripp)

I want the vendor to walk me through, step by step,

what happened that made the contractor "impossible." Listening to the vendor's account will make my understanding concrete and personalized. This will give me a sense of the drama and emotions of the moment.

3   Always ask people to explain why they responded as they did in the examples they gave you. (Why?)

"Now you not only have a definition and a concrete situation, but you can begin to get a little bit of the heart behind the person's behavior. You are asking him to step back and evaluate what was behind the words he said, the choices he made, and the things he did." (Tripp)

As you ask the What, How, and Why questions, you learn the vendor was upset because they delivered materials that did not meet the specifications of the design. The contractor and vendor also had a history where the contractor was already suspicious and untrusting of the vendor from past mistakes on other projects. Because you take the time to the listen and understand by asking him to define, clarify, and explain, you avoid misunderstanding and false assumptions.

Great communication skills start with listening and asking good questions, not talking. Learn how to get others to define, clarify, and explain. Learning this valuable communication skill will help you avoid costly and frustrating misunderstandings.

Challenge

Improving your communication enhances your credibility and increases your trust factor. This Lesson takes practice. Practice asking these questions, "What?," "How?", "Why?" Practice this with your colleagues during the next project meeting. Practice at home with your kids. Practice with your friends during social events. And learn to listen intently after asking your questions.

Lesson 56: Work Habits That Matter

There are work habits that matter more than most. No matter what field of work, industry, or skill, some work habits are consistently appreciated. Many of these are so appreciated, when they are executed consistently, they lead to promotions, raises, and respect!

Responsiveness

Responsiveness is a communication skill that lets colleagues and clients know you have heard their message and how you plan to respond to that message. Responsiveness is appreciated because it demonstrates that you value others before yourself. This skill shows up in how you read and respond to emails, phone messages, texts, and memos. When given a verbal request, those who are responsive repeat the request and write it down, type it into their tasks or their calendar. Responsiveness does not require that you comply with every request or agree to every demand, but it does require that you quickly let the messenger know they have been heard!

Initiative

Initiative is the ability to start or initiate a task without having to be given every step of instruction. It demonstrates the power to act independently and take ownership of a task or project. Initiative is appreciated because it generates trust and confidence from your supervisor or teammates. It feels good to give someone a task with minimal instruction and believe that person will follow through and use their resources and talents to complete the task.

Positive Self-Presentation

Self-Presentation is the way you offer yourself or present yourself for work. This is the impression you give others about what they may expect from you when you are completing a task. You want to present yourself in a way that is positive and will instill confidence in others that you are competent and capable. This is appreciated because it eliminates worry and doubt in your supervisor or teammates while encouraging them that you know what you are doing.

Timeliness

Timeliness is not the same as punctuality. Timeliness is more about being relevant, appropriate, and suitable. Timeliness is about organizing your time and tasks in a way so the most important things get done first. Good timeliness also means not wasting time on trivial or unimportant matters. Timeliness is appreciated because it maximizes your employer's ability to generate profit. After all, timely workers are the most productive workers.

Personal Wellness

Doing your best to eat well, get plenty of sleep and exercise regularly is the core of personal wellness. The simple formula of healthy eating, sleep, and exercise does more for your body and mind than anything else. Your emotional stability, concentration, and sense of purpose are greatly enhanced. Personal wellness is appreciated because it allows you to give your best to yourself and your employer consistently.

If your employer considers you responsive, a self-starter, positive and confident, timely and healthy, you will enjoy job security and be at the top of the list for promotions, raises and respect!

Challenge

What do you need to improve? Which of these work habits do you believe is lacking in you? Do a serious self-examination and be honest with yourself. If you are secure and brave, ask a trusted friend to help you assess these work habits. Be open and willing to take criticism. Once you have your feedback, create a realistic and measurable plan to improve.

For example, if you discover you are not presenting yourself with confidence, find some online training to increase how you are presenting yourself. Consider hiring a life coach to assist you in self-presentation.

Lesson 57: Work Habits That Matter, Part 2

In Part 1, I wrote about five work habits that matter. They were responsiveness, initiative, positive self-presentation, timeliness, and personal wellness. I would like to add a few other habits to this list.

There are work habits that matter more than most. No matter what field of work, industry, or skill, some work habits are consistently appreciated. Many of these are so appreciated, when they are executed consistently, they lead to promotions, raises, and respect!

Thoroughness

Being thorough for some people comes naturally. Engineers, Architects and technically-minded people are usually gifted at being thorough, detailed, meticulous. However, that natural giftedness does not always translate into all areas of work. Being thorough on a set of plans is one thing. Being thorough about reading and responding to emails is another. Being thorough while reviewing a contract is one thing. Being thorough while reading a qualifications proposal is another. What am I saying?

The habit of thoroughness must be cultivated on the things that matter to you as well as the annoying and less interesting responsibilities. And if you are not naturally gifted at being thorough (like me) you must practice it with everything!

Delegating Work

Yes, delegation is a good work habit! Learning how to train others and delegate tasks to them is a valuable work habit. It takes extra time and intention to teach others how to do what you do so well. It takes patience to allow them to make mistakes and learn from those mistakes. However, great leaders model good work and trust those following their leadership to do the same.

When you delegate work tasks to your colleagues and team members, you become more efficient and make room for business growth. When you try to do everything yourself, progress slows, you get stressed, quality suffers, and staff growth stymies.

Communicating Process

Communicating process is about letting others know where you are in the process of delivering requested information or in completing a task. Most never think about communicating process because they do not see the value in it. However, when you communicate process it lets those who are depending on you know that you are working on what they need and whether you are on target or running behind. This is true for both external clients and internal colleagues.

If your employer considers you thorough, able to delegate tasks and a very good communicator, you will enjoy job security and be at the top of the list for promotions, raises and respect!

Challenge

In Part 1 of Work Habits That Matter, I challenged you to self-assess regarding the traits mentioned and ask for feedback. In Part 2, I challenge the same plus one more thing. I am a stickler for communicating process. Because I admit to some hypersensitivity about this subject, I find that

118

most people are very poor at communicating process. If you want to differentiate yourself in the workplace and provide service beyond what most are willing to provide, start learning to communicate your process.

Lesson 58: Execution and Accountability

Every year, we all make New Year's resolutions. According to a Gallup Poll, only 8% follow through on these resolutions and most have given up by January 19. We are remarkably inept at following through on the goals we set for ourselves. So how does the very small minority who do achieve their goals do it? They plan, set accountability, and execute.

The odds of you following through on a goal are 10% at the idea stage, 40% if you set a deadline, 50% if you create a step-by-step plan, and 90% if you utilize accountability partners. If you want to succeed in achieving your goals set deadlines, make a step-by-step plan, and utilize accountability.

When it comes to day-to-day work, most tasks get accomplished because of accountability. If you have five work tasks that must be completed by a specific deadline and you do not accomplish those tasks you run the risk of upsetting your client, making errors, and losing business. These are all strong accountability measures to ensure you complete your goals. But when it comes to "voluntary" tasks and goals such as increasing your business development skills or attending a business networking event, unless you plan and utilize accountability, the odds of you achieving these goals are very small.

If you want to mature in your business acumen and professional development, learn to set specific plans and establish accountability for yourself. The odds of increasing your value to your co-workers and your company goes up tremendously when you plan and set accountability!

Challenge

This challenge is simple. When you have a task you don't like or are not looking forward to completing, make a plan, set deadlines, and make yourself accountable to someone else. If you try to motivate yourself through willpower, the odds of your success are very small. If you employ a trusted colleague or friend to hold you accountable and share you deadline with them, the odds go way up!

Lesson 59: How To Create An Informed Strategy

Strategy is a plan of action designed to achieve a significant goal. An informed strategy is the same plan of action designed with data and information relative to the goal. Here are three ways you can become smarter and more nuanced in your strategic thinking.

1. Recognize that good strategy doesn't have to be innovative. Not every great idea is novel. Many great ideas are simply born from making good choices. Many great ideas come from perfecting someone else's innovation. Strategic thinking is about reviewing and analyzing others' work, the history of what you do, and simply finding different perspectives.

2. Think about future trends in your industry. What is your gut telling you is most likely to happen in the next 5-10 years in your industry or specific niche in which you serve? What is research pointing to or revealing about solutions in your field of work? From these answers, make decisions on how to allocate and invest your time and resources. This type of strategic thinking keeps you ahead of the curve.

3. Make sure you're soliciting input from diverse sources. Get outside of your typical circles of influence and

seek input from unsuspecting sources. When was the last time you collaborated with a client about possible solutions to their problem? Have you ever asked an accountant or your teenage daughter to review an engineering problem? While diverse sources may or may not solve your problem, they will certainly provide different perspectives which can help you solve the problem.

Let your strategic thinking be informed with these three approaches. They can be boiled down into surveying what others are doing, consider the future, and ask for feedback from diverse sources.

Challenge

What area of work responsibility are you currently engaged in that requires strategic thinking? Are you trying to find a way to beat that primary competitor who keeps winning ahead of you? Is it time to refresh your proposal collateral such as resumes, project descriptions, etc.?

Lesson 60: Active Listening

You may not know this, but I am a Licensed Professional Counselor (LPC). This is similar to Professional Engineering (PE) or Architect licenses. Mine is also regulated by the State and requires regular continuing education. I still practice counseling every Friday afternoon via a virtual platform and still have an occasional face-to-face session with a client.

The most important skill of a good counselor is "listening." Good listening requires much more energy and focus than most people realize. Listening is completely different than hearing. I can hear you speaking, but may not have a clue what you are saying because I am not listening. Listening is essential for counseling, but it is also a skill good leaders and consultants practice as well.

I want to introduce you to "active listening." This is a specific type of listening that requires you to pay such close attention in your listening that you can effectively summarize the speaker's message. Active listening captures not only the content of another person's message but understands the emotions and motivations driving their message. Here are the basics of "active listening."

1. Face your speaker directly, shoulders square to their body, eyes locked on their face.

2. Listen in a manner that shows interest and engagement such as an occasional head nod or slight lean in.

3. Allow your speaker to finish their thoughts completely, without interruption.

4. Once the speaker has finished their message, repeat what you heard them say in summary.

5. Ask if you heard them correctly.

These tips help your brain to listen more effectively. The best time to practice active listening is when the conversation is conflicted and laced with negative emotions. Conflict makes active listening very difficult because you may be frustrated, angry, disappointed, or any other number of negative emotions. This makes you defensive and combative. However, practicing active listening in the most difficult conversations will prove to lower the tensions, keep you on track toward a solution and keep you connected to the other person when it is most critical!

Challenge

Assess a recent difficult conversation you have had. Assess the emotions that made that conversation difficult. What were you feeling? How did you respond to those negative feelings? Replay the conversation in your mind.

Did you listen well? Most likely, you would say your listening was not all that good. What would have changed in this conversation had you practiced active listening? How would the conversation have gone if you did not interrupt, if you intently focused on the other person, and weighed their emotions? The best way to change your listening habits is to critically assess past conversations and consider what you would do differently.

Chapter 6 – Writing Skills

Lesson 61: Double Spaced Period

Take a few minutes and Google 'double space after a period.' You will discover the habit you picked up in high school typing class of putting two spaces after a period is no longer necessary. The reason for the original rule of 'double space after a period' had to do with limited type fonts on a typewriter and the way copy looked when typing on a typewriter. Once computer word processing began, the variety of type fonts available exploded. If you will notice when you print copy from a word processing software like Microsoft Word, and you have double spaced after a period, the copy does not look as tight and presentable. To most clients, double spacing after a period tells them you may still be using a typewriter and other antiquated technologies or that you do not stay current with business best practices. Either of those unintended messages can hurt our efforts to win work and keep work.

Do your best to break the habit of double spacing after a period. Even in emails or other digital communication, one space after the period is sufficient.

Challenge

This lesson is somewhat nostalgic for me as it was my very first Monday Marketing Tip email. Little did I know this was the start of a consistent writing project educating my colleagues on best practices in marketing. Rather than challenge you to not double space after the period - which most of you probably already have that one down – I wish to challenge you to start educating your technical colleagues in best marketing practices. Do something consistently that helps your technical staff become better marketers. Even the little things, like single spacing after a period, add up to make big differences over the long haul.

Lesson 62: Writing a Good Cover Letter

Cover letters, or really any letters corresponding with clients, are some of the most important, yet overlooked marketing tools in professional services. A cover letter that introduces your proposal for winning a project may be the single most important piece of the entire proposal. It is like a first impression when meeting with someone in person. If you flub up the first impression, it is very difficult to recover and make a compelling impact.

So, here are a few tips for writing a great cover letter for proposals and qualifications.

1. The first sentence of the first paragraph should be about the client, not you or your firm.

2. If the first sentence is about the client, then it follows that the entire first paragraph should be about the client and their project.

3. Once you have established your understanding of the client and their project, write about a few of the key aspects of the project. Key aspects could be specific challenges, unique features, schedule and budget constraints, project drivers, etc.

4. Differentiate what you are bringing to the client and their project that separates you from the competition.

Differentiators are anything you do that no one else or very few others do. (invoicing detail, specific market expertise, unique in-house skills or knowledge, low overhead, plan production processes, etc.)

5. Summarize what you are giving the client in this specific proposal in the order you are presenting the information.

6. Conclude by repeating your knowledge of the client and their project and answer the ultimate "why?" of what is driving this specific project.

In Appendix D is a sample cover letter for water modeling and an on-call contract for water system engineering. You will notice the primary driver for the project was accelerated growth in the city and their interest in attracting development.

Finally, there are a few parameters in the design and presentation of a good cover letter.

1. Use a font size of 11-point or higher and a simple, easy to read font style.

2. Do your best to limit the cover letter to one page. In special circumstances, a second page may be unavoidable.

3. Use a consistent letterhead that is current and relevant to the office from which the project will be served.

4. Use one-inch left and right margins.

5. Make your cover letter readable; a grade level between 9-11 is ideal. (Word will perform readability statistics on your documents. Google how to use this feature.

Challenge

There are several methods for constructing a great cover letter. Mine is just one of several very good structures. What all great cover letters have in common is the focus on the client and their project, not your firm and your great qualifications. Do a cover letter audit of your firm's letters over the past several years. You will most likely be appalled how often you discover your firm only talking about themselves with very little content regarding the client and project. If you influence the content of your firm's cover letters, resolve to practice putting the client and their project in focus. Use this structure to help guide your efforts.

Lesson 63: Respect Your Readers: Words with Power and Grace

Why is business writing so awful? Have we run out of fresh things to say? Are we too focused on trying to sound professional or smart? Is it the product of an education system that rewards length over clarity?

Business writing would be a lot better if we focused on the reader instead of ourselves. Gracewriting teaches you to write with power by being clear, concise, and correct. We help you write with grace by putting your reader's needs first.

How often have you read proposals/letters/emails that are slammed full of wimpy to-be verbs, endless prepositional phrases, and superfluous, excessive, repeated redundancies? You care about your readers, right? So, let's start putting their needs first by writing concisely and respecting their time. Here's how:

1. Use Strong Verbs: The power of the English language comes from verbs. Tap into that power by replacing wimpy to-be verbs with mighty action verbs. Why "be in agreement with" when you can simply "agree"? Why "make a decision" when you can just "decide"? Strong verbs lead to strong writing!

2. Pass on the Prepositional Idioms: What in the world are prepositional idioms? They are clumps of prepositional phrases that can be replaced with one word. Instead of "in order to," simply use the word "to." Replace "due to the fact that" with "because." Exchange "at this point in time" with "now." Why use several words if one will do?

3. Pull the Word Weeds: Eliminate words that take up space without adding any meaning. Yank up empty sentence openings like "There is" and "It is." Search out redundancies like "past history" or "absolute certainty," and prune those -ly adverbs; "The skillfully executed presentation completely convinced the firm to hire us" is really too much. Remember, every word you write counts!

Respect your audience and their time. Go with less chatter and more substance. The result? Your readers will appreciate you, and you'll land on the shortlist more often!

(this material was written by Jen Hebblethwaite, former Senior VP at Graceworksinc.com)

Challenge

Jen does a wonderful job teaching good writing! This short Lesson is some of her best practices to help your technical staff write well. I challenge you to share these tips with your staff and use these practices in your editing. If you are really ambitious, teach a brief workshop and everyone learns together how to become better writers.

Lesson 64: Change Your Prepositional Idioms

A prepositional idiom is a phrase that can be condensed to one word or eliminated from the sentence. One of the most common problems in poor writing is prepositional idioms. The best way to define this writing issue is to give some examples. The following examples are common prepositional idioms I see in writing project descriptions, approaches, cover letters, etc.

Prepositional Idioms That Begin with a Preposition

In order to, In a timely manner, From day to day, Above all else, For this purpose.

Look for prepositional idioms like these and replace them with one word or delete them. For example, you can change the following sentence, "We will consider safety in design concepts above all else," to "We will consider safety in design concepts first."

One of the most common prepositional idioms I discovered has to do with identifying the project we are discussing. We often use idioms such as for the project, of the project, throughout the project, for this project. Most of the time, these can be eliminated. Consider the following examples.

Example for Condensing a Prepositional Idiom

"Our quality control and assurance measures are executed at every step *throughout the project*."

"Our quality control and assurance measures are executed at every *milestone*."

Example for Eliminating a Prepositional Idiom

"After our scoping meeting, the design team will draft a final scope of work *for the project*."

"After our scoping meeting, the design team will draft a final scope of work."

The reader already knows you are discussing their project. There is no need to qualify your action as being 'of the project' or 'for the project' when the entire document is already discussing their project.

Watch for prepositional idioms in your writing and challenge yourself to condense or eliminate them for better writing.

Challenge

The best method for discovering prepositional idioms is to read your writing out loud. You will notice prepositional idioms repeat, sometimes in the same sentence. You will hear it quicker than you will spot it. Review some of your recent documents and read them out loud. Better yet, have the author (a design professional) read their writing out loud with you. Together, you will both discover the prepositional idioms and unnecessary clauses.

Lesson 65: Use Strong Verbs

Lesson 63 was to Respect Your Reader: Use Words With Power and Grace. One of the tips was to use Strong Verbs. Let us take a deeper dive into using strong verbs in your client letters, emails, and reports.

The power of the English language comes from verbs. Tap into that power by replacing wimpy to-be verbs with mighty action verbs. Why "be in agreement with" when you can simply "agree"? Why "make a decision" when you can just "decide"? Strong verbs lead to strong writing! Here are the most common wimpy verbs and phrases I see most often and the stronger verbs to replace them.

Wimpy	Strong
"In accordance with"	"following" or "per"
"subsequent to"	"after"
"is able to"	"can"
"in order that"	"so"
"in relation to"	"concerning" or "about"
"In light of the fact"	"because" or "due to"
"it is our intention to"	"we intend" or "we will"
"it has come to my attention"	"I noticed"

Take a few extra minutes before sending your letter, email, or report to the client to review for wimpy verb phrases. If you review your writing with an eye for being direct, concise, and active, you will catch these wimpy phrases and verbs.

Challenge

Like the last Lesson's challenge, read your writing out loud. One of the giveaways for wimpy verbs and phrases is when you are reading aloud and it sounds stuffy and academic. For example, read the following sentence out loud;

"It is our intention to study your system in order that we may discover the problems in relation to the overall waste output."

STUFFY! Now let's take out the wimpy verbs and use strong verbs. Read the following out loud;

"We will study your system so we may discover the problems concerning the overall waste output."

So much better!

Lesson 66: Stephen King's Writing Tips

The 'King' of horror novels has a few good writing tips. I believe several of these tips are applicable to professional business writing.

1. Remove everything that is not part of the story. In business writing this is known as 'feature creep.' You set out to define some features of a project and before you know it, you have created a Frankenlist of non-essential features and sub-features. Eliminate what does not drive the main narrative.

2. Do not dress up your vocabulary. Stop puking professional-sounding text on the page. You do not write to

impress others of your intelligence. You write to help others understand and appreciate your work.

3. Avoid adverbs. "I believe the road to hell is paved with adverbs, and I will shout it from the rooftops. To put it another way, they're like dandelions. If you have one on your lawn, it looks pretty and unique. If you fail to root it out, however, you find five the next day ... fifty the day after that ... and then, my brothers and sisters, your lawn is **totally, completely**, and **profligately** covered with dandelions. By then you see them for the weeds they really are, but by then it's—GASP!!—too late." Stephen King

4. Paragraphs are maps of intent. Short paragraphs say, "Come on in, the water's fine!" Long paragraphs say, "Reader beware! This may take a significant commitment." If you want the appearance of your paragraphs to be inviting, keep them short.

5. There is a timeless connection between reading and writing. If you want to write, you need to read. The more well-read you are, the better writer you may become.

If you are interested in the full-length online article, here you go! *Stephen King's Top 13 Writing Tips,* by Bobby Powers | The Writing Cooperative[30]

Challenge

When it comes to writing, practice ... practice ... practice! There is no secret sauce to becoming a great writer overnight. When you look at a prolific writer like Stephen King and discover his writing tips are simple and straightforward, you discover writing really is just practice. I challenge you to find opportunities to write regularly. Just like this book, it started with me writing a Monday Morning Marketing tip every week for over a year. I stayed dedicated to the process of writing consistently. I created an obligation for myself. Keep writing!

Lesson 67: Work Harder At Writing Better

As a technical or design professional, you often write reports, letters, emails, proposals, memos and more. Writing is a critical piece of your everyday work. Good writing supports good communication, both internally with colleagues and externally with clients and business partners. Here are a few tips on strengthening your writing.

Use Lists.

When writing a series of steps or explaining a process, use lists. Rather than write long sentences full of multiple steps or items, break them out into a brief list. For example, rather than writing, "To initiate the project we will perform a kick-off meeting, define the project scope, collect data, start preliminary planning, define funding sources, develop plans and specifications, coordinate with regulating agencies, assist with bidding, finalize a construction contract, and provide construction representation," Write a list like this, "To initiate the project we will …

a. Perform a kick-off meeting,

b. Define the project scope,

c. Collect data,

d. Start preliminary planning,

e. Define funding sources,

f. Develop plans and specifications,

g. Coordinate with regulating agencies,

h. Assist with bidding,

i. Finalize a construction contract,

j. Provide construction representation.

Write To A Lower Grade Level

You have an Editor feature with Microsoft Word that has the option to give you readability statistics. Go to "File"

"Options" "Proofing" and check the "Show Readability Statistics" box. Your ideal grade level should be between 9-11. This can sometimes be a challenge with technical writing but can be accomplished with practice. Writing that lowers the grade level includes shorter sentences and shorter words. So rather than writing, "It is our understanding," write "we understand."

Read Your Piece Aloud

Reading your piece aloud helps you hear what your readers will hear. This is the easiest way to catch run-on or complex sentences. You will often discover typos and punctuation mistakes when reading aloud.

These are just a few tips on making your writing stronger. Stronger writing leads to better communication and happier colleagues and clients. Make yourself easier to work with by improving your writing.

Challenge

Take several project descriptions or approaches you wrote and re-write them using these three tips. Where can you change long sentences with multiple steps into a list? Write in a Word document and run the readability statistics on your writing. Keep editing until you get to a grade level of 11 or lower. Read the whole thing aloud and make adjustments so it sounds right in your speaking voice.

Lesson 68: 7 Deadly Sins of Proposal Writing

The Simplar Foundation is a group of researchers and procurement specialists who focus on improving an organization's "ability to operate, better meet the public need, implement best practices, and more effectively train the workforce." (www.simplarfoundation.org)

In their research regarding A/E/C industry procurement, they've uncovered some typical 'cut and paste' language to avoid. Their analysis of 71 contractor proposals containing both successful and unsuccessful bids revealed that procurement committees did not respond well to the cut-and-paste marketing language that contractors used in their proposals. Their research uncovered the seven deadly phrases that contractors would cut and paste from one proposal to another:

1. *"We will work with the Client to …"* or *"We will meet with the Client to …"* or *"We will collaborate with the Client to…"*

2. "We have XX years of experience …"

3. *"We use the best pre-qualified list of subs, suppliers, and manufacturers…"*

4. *"We are highly experienced in"*… (insert current industry buzzword, i.e. Lean, JIT, BIM, LEED, sustainability, etc.)

5. *"Our company values are…* (insert company mission statement, i.e., *"We use a Total Team Approach™"*)

6. *"Our people are our greatest asset…"*

7. *"Safety is our #1 priority…"*

When writing a cover letter, proposal or project approach, look for these phrases and their variations in your writing. When you spot them, delete them and think of something better to say. When in doubt, write about the client's project, their organizational objectives, what your solution to their specific problem will look like.

Challenge

It is time to take a brutal look at some key pieces of your recent proposals. Take the seven phrases in this lesson and search for these phrases or similar in your proposals. When you find them, think of something else you could say instead. If you have trouble thinking of better things to say, here are a few suggestions.

1. You own this project. Therefore, we seek and value your input and collaboration.

2. Your project is very familiar and contains many similarities to projects we have completed.

3. A successful project requires exceptional communication between all parties, including sub-contractors, vendors and manufacturers.

4. There are many technical tools and methodologies we employ to deliver a successful project. Together, we will help you discover which of these will work best.

5. We value collaboration, communication, and safety.

6. You will enjoy the professionalism and expertise our staff embodies. We are well-trained and skilled in …

7. Every construction project must prioritize safety.

Lesson 69: Bug Dust

Bug dust are the elements of a proposal or statement of qualifications that have "**no significant influence on whether you win the job or not.**" Did you read that first part slowly and intentionally? *No significant influence!*

Bug dust is …

• Should we use contractions in the proposal? Isn't that too informal?

• Do we always need to "thank the client for the opportunity?"

• Is there too much "whitespace?" Shouldn't we fill up the page?

• When we write P.E. do we need the periods or can we just write PE?

• Should we put our logo here? What about here?

Here are the most important elements of a proposal or statement of qualifications. This is what we should focus our time and attention on.

o The deadline! Meet your deadlines for content so there is time for quality review and editing.

o Write a great cover letter. Cover letters are the most read page and usually read entirely.

o Focus on budget and schedule. These are almost always the two most important details to the client.

o Place priority focus on project experience and technical qualifications that matter to that specific project.

Let's put aside the bug dust and focus on what will win more work! Want better proposals? Stop worrying about bug dust! (helpeverybodyeveryday.com)[31]

Challenge

Find the bug dust and eliminate it! When the conversations over proposals start heading into the bug dust weeds, be courageous enough to stop it. It is okay to say, "that really doesn't matter."

True Story. My company recently submitted qualifications in consideration of an on-call city engineering contract. According to the go/no-go process, we had a very high chance of winning the contract. We had successful past projects. We knew about the RFQ well before it was issued. We had several meaningful conversations with the administration and a few city council members. I actually sit on a community development board with the City Administrator. However, after turning in the qualifications package, I realized we misspelled … wait for it … *the name of the city … on the front cover*!

We still won the contract. Why? Because the bug dust does not matter.

Lesson 70: Short Words Are Better Than Long Words

When it comes to marketing content, we take lessons from the best-selling novelists. Did you know that best sellers of any genre have 4.5 letters-per-word or fewer? Most were fewer than 4.3. In fact, the lower it was, the better the seller. Said another way, you should use short words if you want people to read what you write.

However, as engineers and design professionals, you were trained to write using large words and industry jargon. Like writing at an eighth- to tenth-grade level, using smaller words helps your readers. When you use gigantic audacious words in long run on sentences that produce in the reader the necessity to have to decipher the sentence more than a few times before conquering its subject matter, you become unintelligible. Or, when you use big words in long sentences it causes the reader to work too hard.

Why say 'utilize' when you can say 'use?' Instead of 'perform,' use 'do.' Rather than 'inception,' use 'start.' Say 'move' instead of 'relocate.'

As Mark Twain once said, "Why should I write 'metropolis' when I get paid the same for 'city'?"

Challenge

Use your readability statistics editor in Word. Work on writing content that stays below an 11th grade level. One of the best ways to bring the grade level down is to replace big words with smaller ones. Trying to sound smart is no way to help your readers. Help them by making the complex simple.

About the Author

Gabe Lett has been marketing A/E/C services since 2003. He began with his father's civil engineering firm performing marketing tasks part-time. This grew into a passion and career change from a mental health counseling practice to a full-time marketing career in 2009. Since that time Gabe has served three different engineering companies in marketing and business development. Gabe is a Fellow of the Society for Marketing Professional Services and a Certified Professional Services Marketer. He has written articles for several trade journals and has presented at regional and national conferences for A/E/C marketers.

Gabe and his family live in Southwest Missouri. Chief among the many outdoor activities he enjoys are his annual mountaineering trips to Colorado. Gabe volunteers for his local church, community, and school serving in several leadership roles and boards. Above all, Gabe is a devout follower of Jesus. His love for Jesus fuels all his activities and is the foundation from which his life is lived.

Appendix A

Sample Client Email (Chapter 3, Lesson 32)

Subject Line: Water Treatment Plant Owner's Rep for Design Build

Body: Greetings Monty, Bill & Susan,

I left a voice message for Susan today regarding your upcoming Water Treatment Plant project. We are interested in speaking with you about the Owner's Representative role for this significant water plant project. We are performing a very similar role for Perryville, MO for a new wastewater treatment plant constructed by a Design/Build team. Our team is available to visit virtually Monday or Tuesday of next week, November 16 or 17.

Please indicate if those dates may work or suggest an alternative. Thank you for your consideration!

Signature

Appendix B

Project Completion Form (Chapter 4, Lesson 40)

Engineer's Project Completion Form

(Please submit to the Marketing Department upon completion of your project.)

Name of Project

_____

Project Type

Reference Contact Name and Title

City/State   Phone #   Email

Project Writeup

Reason for Project/Problem Client Needed Solved:

Solution:

Features of the Project: (Technical specs, engineering data, etc.)

Project Bid Price $_____

Final Price $_____

Change   _____%

Appendix C

Project Follow-Up Email Template (Chapter 4, Lesson 41)

Subject: Project Success Conversation Request

Dear Client,

(Appreciation)

Thank you for the opportunity to work with you on [project name.] My team and **I have enjoyed the experience**, and we're glad to hear from your feedback that you've found success in the project as well.

(Value)

I would like to schedule a time to **talk about your success**, and what things we are doing specifically that help. It's critical to us that we don't take success for granted, and that we carefully examine how to continue achieving for you in our quest to always improve.

(Hope)

We heard you say that [something positive from their feedback] is **making an impact**, and that's just one area we can investigate.

(Enjoyment)

Could we **perhaps meet for lunch** on [date options], or find a time in your office or via phone to connect?

Thank you very much for helping us be our best,

[Signature]

Appendix D

Sample Cover Letter (Chapter 6, Lesson 62)

Date

Mr. Fictitious Name, Public Works Director

Fictitious Address

City, State Zip Code

Re: RFQ Water Distribution Network Model

Mr. Fictitious Name & Selection Committee,

We love what "Fictitious City" is doing! From the revitalization of downtown with Block 22 to the Develop City Housing Campaign, "Fictitious City" is positioning itself to grow. As your neighbors, we have observed the City for a long time. "Firm Name" has always taken an interest in partnering with "Fictitious City" for your on-going growth and improvement. We recognize that with your new investment in leadership and initiatives to develop, now is a great time to join forces. Adding our professional engineering staff to your stable of talent will send a message that you are serious about making "Fictitious City" a great place to live, work and play.

One of the most critical elements to attracting new business and industry is the quality, availability, and affordability of clean water. Your ability to deliver clean water and fire suppression at a reasonable cost can be a significant differentiator in attracting new business and industry. This also impacts your ISO Rating which factors into all development; industrial, commercial, and residential. Investing in your water infrastructure is one of the primary ways to attract the growth you desire.

Creating a water model and understanding the dynamics of your water operations is one of our greatest strengths. To model your system, we consider many factors to assist in your decisions for improvements. Our goal is to provide you with the most accurate data and help interpret that data to assess future demand, identify deficiencies, evaluate proposed development, and various scenarios of change to the system. We want "Fictitious City" to be equipped with the right knowledge to make the best and most cost-effective decisions for your water system.

Beyond the initial water model, we want to be a reliable resource for continued water system decisions. Your decision is not just about choosing the right firm for a water model. It is also about a longer-term relationship with a professional who can listen and work with City leaders to help you reach your ultimate goals of attracting growth and development. The staff we offer you in this qualifications document are long-tenured experts who wish to be a reliable resource for the long-term.

You will learn in this document our approach to completing this work, the modeling software we utilize, our team and their water system proficiency, our deep bench of completed similar projects, and a proposed schedule for completion. And one more thing!

We would love to work for the "Fictitious City" and be a part of your great success!

References

[1] Scott D. Butcher, FSMPS, CPSM, www.aecumen.com

[2] Scott D. Butcher, FSMPS, CPSM, "Marketing 2022: A Survey Exploring Current and Future A/E/C Marketing Practices."

[3] Amazon.com: The Collapse of Distinction: Stand Out and Move Up While Your Competition Fails (9781595551856): McKain, Scott: Books

[4] Update – my firm ended 2020 with a 51% hit rate, the highest since they began tracking hit rates.

[5] Update – we launched our firm's first blog platform in 2021. AM In The AM (amce.com)

[6] "Procurement of Architecture and Engineering Services: Influence of Cost on Selection Outcomes and Evaluation Criteria That Best Differentiate Consultant Expertise" Brian C. Lines, Ph.D, M.ASCE and Amirali Shalwani

[7] Building a StoryBrand: Clarify Your Message So Customers Will Listen: Miller, Donald: 9780718033323: Amazon.com: Books

[8] https://www.cnbc.com/2018/10/12/mark-cuban-one-of-the-most-underrated-business-skills-is-being-nice.html

[9] https://www.mindtools.com/pages/article/newCDV_59.htm

[10] https://www.inc.com/john-hall/these-6-mistakes-can-undermine-your-leadership.html?

[11] Scott D. Butcher, FSMPS, CPSM, "Marketing 2022: A Survey Exploring Current and Future A/E/C Marketing Practices."

[12] https://kinsta.com/blog/linkedin-statistics/

[13] "How to Earn the Role of Trusted Advisor," Michael Buell, FSMPS, Assoc. DBIA SMPS-Marketer-eBook-Business-Development-FINAL.pdf

[14] Overcoming-Seven-Leadership-Thinking-Traps_Marketer-June-2020.pdf (smps.org)

[15] Rain Making: Attract New Clients No Matter What Your Field: Harding, Ford: 9781598695885: Amazon.com: Books

[16] Make them want what you do! – The Zweig Letter

[17] Long-term results – The Zweig Letter

[18] "The Entire Business Development Process in 11 Words" Michael T. Buell, FSMPS, CPSM, Assoc. DBIA (Marketer, October, 2019)

[19] 7 Best Practices for Managing Client Relationships Effectively (hubspot.com)

[20] "Can an Introvert Succeed at BD? (Yes, Here's How)" by Rich Friedman, (Marketer Journal, October, 2018)

[21] Seven-Things-Your-Clients-Want-You-To-Know_Marketer-June-2020.pdf (smps.org)

[22] Measuring Success With the Loyalty Ladder - SMPS

[23] The Win Without Pitching Manifesto: Blair Enns: 9781605440040: Amazon.com: Books

[24] Research - SMPS The Neuropsychology of Influence and Decision-Making, Jonrobert Tartaglione

[25] Managing expectations – The Zweig Letter

[26] Pricing Creativity, a Revolutionary Book on Value-Based Pricing (winwithoutpitching.com)

[27] No More Oughts and Shoulds! - Graceworks (graceworksinc.com)

[28] https://www.inc.com/larry-kim/the-differences-between-busy-productive-people.html?cid=sf01003&sr_share=facebook

[29] Instruments in the Redeemer's Hands: People in Need of Change Helping People in Need of Change (Resources for Changing Lives): Paul David Tripp: 9780875526072: Amazon.com: Books

[30] Stephen King's Top 13 Writing Tips | by Bobby Powers | The Writing Cooperative

[31] Want Better Proposals? Stop Worrying About Bug Dust! (helpeverybodyeveryday.com)

.

www.ingramcontent.com/pod-product-compliance
Lightning Source LLC
Chambersburg PA
CBHW070931210326
41520CB00021B/6890

9 780578 304526